Benjamin Bonetti Ltd
First published in Great Britain 2010
By Benjamin P. Bonetti
www.benjaminbonetti.com

© Benjamin Bonetti Ltd 2010. All rights reserved. No part of this publication may be reproduced, stored in a retrieval system, or transmitted, in any form or by any means, without the prior permission in writing of the publisher, nor be otherwise circulated in any form of binding or cover other than that which it is published and without a similar condition including this condition being imposed on the subsequent purchaser.

Every effort has been made to trace copyright owners. Please notify Benjamin Bonetti Ltd of any omissions and they will be rectified

Dedicated to my father
Philip Bonetti and my
children

Acknowledgements

"Time is our most valuable asset, yet we tend to waste it, kill it, and spend it rather than invest it." Jim Rohn

Not one person can give, have or be anything without the assistance of others. Although the information within this book is based on personal experiences; I would like to give special thanks to so many people for their continued dedication to personal development, change therapy and those who have positively influenced my life.

Each of the following people has added directly to the building this fantastic business resource:

Philip Bonetti (My Father) - for being there when I needed the truth, support and guidance.

My Children (Joseph & Emiliana) – for expecting nothing but giving everything.

Training Cpl Royal Engineers (you know who) – for "can't means won't, won't means head butt".

Mr. K. Keast MBE – for believing that I was good enough and for many wise words.

Tony Robbins, Paul McKenna, Richard Bandler – setting the benchmark for mass personal development, a goal to which I aspire.

Terry Elston – for just being Terry, and introducing me into the world of NLP.

Debra Swinley – the proof is in the pudding, thanks for being a superstar.

Contents

Chapter		Page
1	**Getting Honest**	1
	What Do You Want In Business - Money, Fulfilment, Recognition?	3
	Anyone Can Be Rich; It's Just A Mindset	10
	Can You Deliver As An Entrepreneur?	15
	Do You Know Your Market And Do They Know You?	18
	Is It The Best Business For You?	21
	What Do You Personally Have To Offer?	24
	Are You Strong Enough Mentally And Physically?	26
	Why Is Now The Right Time?	28
2	**Getting Started**	33
	Forget A Business Plan - A Cigarette Packet Is Good Enough!	35
	How Big Is Big? - Conquering The World!	41
	Get The Professionals Behind You - The Extra Crutch	46
	You Don't Need A Ferrari - What Are The Basics?	50
	The Bank - Who's Got The Money?	53
	Get Educated - Learn The Mistakes Of Others By Reading Daily	59
	Procrastinating Promise - The Best Time To Start Was Last Year	61
3	**Research - Get On With It!**	67
	Tell Everyone! - They Help You, You Help Yourself	69
	Who Are Your Clients? No Really, Who You Are Your Clients?	74
	Where Do They Go And What Do They Eat?	77
	The Chameleon In You - You Like Mickey Mouse? So Do I!	80

Contents

Chapter	Page
4 Building A Business, Not An Income	**87**
Sustainable Business Planning – Allocate Monthly Time	89
Selling To The Next Generation – Talk To Teachers And Parents	93
Affiliate Schemes – Sell Yourself, Products And Services	94
Don't Borrow, Save – Invest In Your Business Monthly	100
Create More Income Streams – Sell Your Competitor's Products	103
How Are They Going To Remember You? – Trusted Consultant!	105
Time Isn't Free And It Doesn't Help The Cash Flow	109
5 Know Your Product Or Service	**113**
Is Your Product Better, Worse Or Different?	115
Know The Difference Between Price And Value	122
Get Feedback – Testimonials Provide Power!	126
Ask Your Clients What They Want Next	130
Its Only Got To Be 10% Better Than The Others	133
6 Magical Money	**137**
What Is Money And Why Do You Want It?	139
Selling At A Profit Is Easy When You Have The Internet!	143
Clients That Pay Late vs. Clients Who Pay On Time!	146
Up-Selling And Cross-Selling – Good And Bad Practices	150
Still Keep The Door Open Even If There's A Draft	152
7 Marketing & Advertising	**157**
The Right Image – Professional, Poor or Peasant	159
Mission Statement – Creating Your Final Legacy	163

Contents

Chapter	Page
Attention Interest, Desire Action – Stop And Think	165
Stop Paying, Start Blogging – Website Essentials	169
PR – Adding Value To Your Market	173
Face To A Name – Name To A Face	177

8	**There Is No Such Thing As Luck**	**183**

Lucky People Start At 6, Finish At 10	185
The Support - Getting Someone Better To Do It	189
Spend Less, Sell More – Bigger Margins, Bigger Balance	191
The Inevitable Feeling Of Being Alone – Home Life	195
Manage Your Mind, Manage Your Business	200
Wealth Is Good, So Enjoy It! – Make Happiness A Present	202
Rewarding Yourself For Doing Good – Smile!	205
Put Something Back – Share Your Knowledge With Others	206

Not The End But The Beginning	**209**
Benjamin's Top Tips To Being An Effective Entrepreneur	211

Foreword

"The real voyage of discovery consists not in making new landscapes but in having new eyes." Marcel Proust

Like most entrepreneurs who reflect upon their past; my own quest for excellence was propelled by Three Key Motivators; to which I owe my success, fulfilment and happiness.

Looking back to my childhood, I was very excitable and always the first person to ask "Why?" I wanted to know why people acted a certain way or why they did the things they did. Most importantly, I wanted to know what drove people to do the things they do. The First Motivator that I can remember occurred during my time at school. Although a fairly academic student, I failed to find the motivation to apply myself and preferred the easier route of not doing something. Looking back I now realize that I spent more time avoiding the task than if I were to actually have done it. This may sound familiar to many people when recalling their youth.

During a secondary school lesson with a frustrated teacher, I remember him saying: "Bonetti, you will amount to nothing, be nothing and end up like the rest of the academic drop-outs from your year!" Accepting this tirade as a chance to prove him wrong, and shortly after receiving his predicted less than adequate GCSE's, I applied to the local Sixth Form College.

This is where the Second Motivator came from; during the initial entrance interview at the College. It was explained that unfortunately, due to failing to meet the minimum entry standards, I would have to spend the following year re-sitting what I had just learnt!

Armed with the second setback, I took massive action and called my father and asked him to take me to the Army Career's Office. Within the following six months my application was processed and I was on my way to Arborfield Apprentice College. Over the following several years, I was fortunate enough to travel across the world, playing rugby at Corp level including several games in Canada. I spent 10 months in Northern Ireland with the historic regiment of The Coldstream Guards; whilst meeting some fantastic and inspirational people.

After attending an Officer's Development Programme, I decided that although the military offered a fantastic future, abundant in opportunities, I would never truly achieve my lifelong goal of owning my own business. I left the army within the same year at the age of 22.

Now armed with a long line of discipline, project management and the so-called important civilian qualifications; including an exemplary military conduct, I was confident that I would be fighting employers off! My job application campaign started with over 100 applications sent. I thought that it was just a matter of time until the phone rang off its hook! Over the following months letters advising me of unsuccessful applications for positions arrived. But there were no interviews and not a single offer of employment. This is the point in time where the Third Motivator happened.

Although I was now more than qualified to hold a senior management position, my age to experience ratio was dramatically weighted. I was stunned when an interviewer said that I was: "over-qualified and under-aged". At that critical moment I was employed at the "Bella Vista" (a friend's parent's restaurant) washing dishes, that was when I made a personal vow that no one would ever tell me what I couldn't do.

From that point I have never looked back. My journey over the last 10 years can be looked back upon with a sense of pride and achievement. I established "Estate Agents" with a good friend Paul, and sold it several months later. I have gone from owing £250,000 to earning a substantial income. I married my childhood sweetheart and fathered two fantastic children. I established my personal development company, Benjamin Bonetti Ltd; and most importantly created internal fulfilment.

My personal legacy is: "Inspiring others to achieve great things".

This book is part of that legacy… so thank you and I hope you enjoy!

1 - Getting Honest

1 Getting Honest

What Do You Want in Business – Money, Fulfilment, Recognition?

Being in business for yourself can often be tricky, especially when things get tough. But it can also bring financial freedom, fulfilment and recognition in abundance. I love my business and so should you!

I wish I had a pound for every time someone asked me what makes an entrepreneur, what my tips are and how they should go about creating a life of abundance. Within this book I will attempt to answer the questions I faced when starting out and reveal the tips I have learnt along the way to assist you in your journey as a entrepreneur.

> **FACT**
>
> American Airlines saved £40,000 in 1987 by eliminating one olive from each salad served in first class.

The first stepping stone and the most valuable recommendation for success is to establish what you really want out of your business and decide if "business" is the right vehicle to achieving those outcomes. A simple recommendation I know, but having worked with many business owners from small enterprises to multimillion pound corporations, few senior management and business owners actually have a clear understanding of what they are aiming for. Believe it or not, how you answer this question actually plays a fundamental part in the approach and direction that you are taking subconsciously, not only within your business but your whole life, and probably one of the reasons you picked up this book.

How? Well think about it for a moment, your business decisions will differ based on that answer and your success or failure will count on it. A question that I ask college students when talking about "career and education direction" that can easily show the importance of direction is:

"Where would you go if you got in your car and started driving without knowing a destination or the purpose of a trip? Would you stay still on your drive or would you go and see where life took you? How long would it be before you got bored and decided to head home? Would you know how to get back without a map? Where would you end up? At what stage would you consider yourself lost?"

You should ask yourself before setting out on your journey within business; can you run a successful business without knowing what you hope to achieve or knowing your destination? Of course not; in fact it's the one question that entrepreneurs need to answer with complete certainty and clarity. Like most things in life, I believe you'll never notice what you're looking for until you know what it is you want.

ASK YOURSELF

 What do you really want out of your business within one month, one year, five years, and ten years?

 When do you want this business venture to end and what do you want to achieve?

If you're thinking of starting a business, and looking for some pointers on how to be a successful entrepreneur, then stop here. Spend the same amount of time answering this question as you would spend writing your business plan. It will make the business plan make more sense, flow and you'll be able to deliver it with more enthusiasm and confidence. If you already own a business, then establish this first before moving on. If you need to, think back to the reasons why you started your business in the first place and establish if you're still on that path to achieving those goals or outcomes. If you're not then don't procrastinate about it, simply reset your destination and remind yourself more often.

Avoid making the fundamental mistake of starting a business without giving much thought to what you want out of it. All too often I am introduced to aspiring business owners, looking for quick fix solutions to their business dilemmas. Unfortunately the majority of these unsuccessful business owners share the same story (strategy). At some stage in their past, after having enough of their previously employed position, they have enthusiastically taken the big leap into business without giving much thought as to the reason! Although bagged with an abundance of enthusiasm, they naively think that they know all they need to, or believe that a client would like their new and innovative idea or perhaps even a niche; this is not enough.

While there is something to be said for positive thinking and spontaneity in business, not knowing your direction can create an avalanche of failures, and I strongly believe that this is the main reason why so many businesses fail unnecessarily. In my World, you must know what you want in business and know the reasons why! This is your roadmap to success, without it you're going to get lost.

TOP TIPS

 Whenever you are making a big decision, stop and question why you are doing it.

 Dig deep until you find the absolute answer to the question; make sure you understand the answer fully on an emotional level.

 Trust your gut feelings about your abilities and only continue when it feels absolutely right.

One simple but effective tool that has determined my path and can help you understand the importance and *direction* of your business, is to take a few hours out of your business (away somewhere where you will not be disturbed) and create a statement. This is commonly known as a mission statement. The mission statement I created when starting out within the personal development profession (still in place to date) is: "Inspiring others to achieve great things". Although it fits nicely within our business/industry and works well as a tag line, it most importantly reminds colleagues and our clients of what we are jointly working towards and what we aim to achieve within our business.

If you are thinking about creating a statement for your business right now or have not got around to doing it yet, think of it as the beating heart of the business, the core, something that is going to be around longer than you and your clients. This will push limitations about what you think you can achieve and open up your mind to learning new *learnings*. Make sure you can say your mission statement with passion and enthusiasm.

FACT

Bill Bowerman, the co-founder of the shoe company Nike, got his first shoe idea after staring at a waffle iron. This gave him the idea of using squared spikes to make the shoes lighter.

It's very important to get this statement "right" first time, so spend some quality time establishing what you really want. Although it's simply a statement to most, it will give you confidence and motivation in your purpose as an entrepreneur. At times this can be reassuring, especially when doubting and making difficult decisions. Within my own business I remember being at crossroads, being fearful of which direction to take, both paths ultimately lead to success but both offered completely different outcomes. By referring back to the mission statement, I had clarity of thought and made the right decision based on the outcome which achieved the best connection with the statement.

This powerful statement should not be taken for granted as it can align everyone within your business and discourages those clients who don't have the same objective, and most importantly, acts as an effective guidance system for you.

TOP TIPS

 If you haven't got a business/lifetime mission then think about your business/life and what you would like to be known for.

 Make sure that everyone knows your mission and perhaps incorporate this mission within your branding.

One of the things that I enjoy about being a business speaker is the fascinating stories that you hear about why people have started their businesses. Over the years I have heard thousands that make sense and more that don't. Having studied many on each side, there is a common factor in both, which can be guaranteed on every occasion. The reason for most entrepreneurs to go into business, no matter how individual they are, will always fall into one of the following motivational categories.

These motivational categories are often referred to within my seminars as the key motivational triggers for achieving success; and simply set out a clear reason what you expect/hope to achieve by being in business. Although often misunderstood and criticized by critics for being shallow or vain, these motivational triggers are fundamental assets in being a highly motivated entrepreneur and a successful business owner.

Trigger 1 - Money Motivation:

Yes it's a fact; some entrepreneurs are solely in business to make money. From my experience these entrepreneurs are fantastic when it comes to obtaining wealth, but have several weaknesses. They are rarely fulfilled by their daily activities, and as a result any mundane tasks will tend to be left as they start a completely new venture. They have problems getting ventures finished unless they see an immediate monetary return, and even if they do they will be always looking for the "next big thing" before the task is completed. The "thought" of receiving a big cheque is the key motivator within this entrepreneur, with constant aspirations to achieve more. Money in the eyes of this person solves all problems. However, although they are driven by money and have fantastic visualisation abilities, they can often lack a respect for it and regularly fall into a trap of yoyo wealth. They go from abundance to nothing, and will continue on this cycle until the pain outweighs the gain.

Trigger 2 - Fulfilment Motivation:

Some entrepreneurs are solely in business because they want to feel more emotionally fulfilled in life, and why not! This type of motivation is what I believe is the most common reason why entrepreneurs exist. This entrepreneur often sets off in their chosen career working for someone else and is later motivated to leave and establish their own business. They generally "believe" that running their own business is a means to achieving emotional fulfilment and happiness and are on most occasions right. Fulfilment in this sense is felt with the idea fuelled by the thought of criticism, with influential people within their past generally doubting their ability to achieve. This type of entrepreneur although a extremely hard worker, can often spend years looking for the right business and can miss fantastic financial opportunities. They base business decisions on how it feels on an emotional level, not on a logical.

Trigger 3 -Recognition Motivation:

The third group of entrepreneurs often solely work for recognition. Although from experience in the minority, they still exist. There are many theories about this type of entrepreneur in the "psychotherapy world". Broadly speaking, the idea is that they didn't receive much recognition when they were younger and seek recognition though achievement within their business. I believe this antiquated idea has changed slightly and although may be true in some cases, falls more in line with the modern ideological "fame and celebrity status" portrayed by the media. This type of entrepreneur often plans carefully and can deal with adversity easier than the others; but can be clouded by the motivational trigger and can fail to recognize the importance of people within their business.

So which one sounds like you and what is the secret? Who are the most successful of the three? Over the years I have been very fortunate to work with and study hundreds of fantastic entrepreneurs, some are continuing to earn millions and others are still in the process. Although they are all extremely talented people, the most successful entrepreneurs have mastered the art of using a mixture of all three motivators. In other words they want all three. Going against the grain of many critics; there's nothing wrong with being rich, famous and happy. In fact, it's better to be all three.

You should think about it this way: money, in itself, is not evil or bad. Of course unethically gaining money will never work. Being motivated to do well and create more wealth and abundance in your life is a good goal to work towards. Wanting better things for yourself and your family is a respectable pursuit and you should be proud of it.

> **FACT**
>
> Close to fifty percent of Internet shoppers spend over five hours a week online.

The idea of needing fulfilment during your success journey is equally as important as making money. Anyone can have money if they work more hours, increase savings and are creative. It's the simple rule of life. However, it's making money and filling that gap of fulfilment which is essential. I believe that you'll never give your business the best chances of success if you don't truly love your work, hence the importance of knowing why and what you want!

Being fulfilled by your business is more important than many business owners recognize. It acts as a huge leverage point (motivation) when things get tough; especially when you're doing something that you rather you wouldn't. You'll be more likely to put in those couple of extra hours if you enjoy doing what you're doing.

The final cornerstone is recognition. While some entrepreneurs will completely deny the fact that they enjoy and desire recognition; it is innate within the human spirit to want to be recognized for our accomplishments, and this isn't wrong. When you do something good, you want someone to notice. It's as simple as that. If you think back to your childhood, you wanted your parents to praise you for doing well or good behaviour. No matter what age we are, we will always need recognition and a sense of accomplishment. It's part of being human. Recognition can often give you the boost to continue when times are tough or the pat on the back when you need it.

Your ultimate aim of being an entrepreneur should be to have money, fulfilment and recognition; but also to be proud of to striving to make your life and the lives of others better.

Anyone Can Be Rich; It's Just A Mindset

My father has always been a massive influence within my life and often the first person I call upon when business is going well or when it's reached a hurdle. His trusted advice over the years has been at the forefront of my mission and assisted my business ventures to grow.

One year when I was about 12 years old, we were holidaying at the family house in Locarno, Switzerland. He sat me down and gave me a piece of advice that has influenced my thinking above all else:

He said: *"Imagine life as a big theme park and within that theme park are two different types of people. There are those who like the gentle cup and saucers and those who like the fast rollercoasters. The people who like the cups and saucers generally like routine and they find security in knowing where they are going and where they have been. Those who like the rollercoasters live for the moment and enjoy the highs, but know around the corner is going to be some lows. If you choose the rollercoaster, and it's your choice, then be prepared as once the ride has started it's going to be tough to get off."* - Philip Bonetti

Although it's not a scientific analysis on society, this piece of theory kicked-started my mission from an early age to discover what separated the super wealthy from those who end up living in the poorest situations, struggling to find the money to buy the basic needs. I couldn't understand why most people given the choice would choose the cups and saucers over the rollercoaster! Surely the adrenaline of the rollercoaster outweighed the dullness of the cups and saucers?

After evaluating my past and the key influential people within it, I noticed that for many of my teen years, I incorrectly assumed like most people that success had something to do with your type of background, how well you spoke or even your IQ. This slightly restrictive way of thinking wasn't influenced by my family or friends but by my senior school teachers; and their inherited idea of how they thought that wealth could be achieved. I can even remember now a teacher saying: "Without good education results you cannot achieve anything or get a good job."

Although education is massively important and should be taken seriously, within my initial research I discovered story after story of people who were raised in challenging situations, without education or support. Who ended up becoming multimillionaires and in some cases even billionaires. These people, who against all odds believed in themselves, believed in their right for success and therefore achieved their dream.

To briefly name a few of the most renowned: Russia's richest man and astute business man Roman Abramovich, was an orphan. Apple's iconic Steve Jobs was adopted and is said to have dropped out of college when he couldn't pay the fees. The world's wealthiest and most fantastic novelist, J.K. Rowling, was on welfare raising her little girl when her agent called to tell her, that her book *Harry Potter* would be published.

This discovery contradicted everything that I had been taught in the past and I couldn't understand why. Why would people be taught something when it wasn't the truth or even close to it. So the question is: If education, background or family support isn't the deciding factor, then what is and what does separate these people from the majority? What gives people the motivation to take the bull by the horns and go for it?

> *The secret to being a successful entrepreneur is "attitude".*

Although it's not the most inspirational of one liner's, and you could find many other more elaborate theories on the Internet, in my World it couldn't be any simpler. The more you start to tune and focus your mind to success, the faster you'll start to notice success. While that may seem so simplistic, it really isn't that hard.

When you study the lives of successful entrepreneurs, you'll discover that there is a direct relationship between their success, their attitude, their internal language and their vision. The right attitude and vision is essential in becoming a successful entrepreneur.

> **FACT**
>
> When Scott Paper Co. first started manufacturing toilet paper they did not put their name on the product because of embarrassment.

Whether you are building your business or changing the dynamics of your enterprise, it is extremely important that you take your attitude very seriously. The way you think about your business and yourself will greatly affect whether or not your business will survive.

I would recommended researching the principals of The Law of Attraction. While some people consider it to be an almost spiritual concept, entrepreneurs that understand what The Law of Attraction actually means, achieve incredible results. I, for one, think the theory is a great resource for aligning your mind.

> **"You become what you think about"**
>
> - Earl Nightingale

In a nutshell, the principle of The Law of Attraction simply states that creating positive energy and positive thoughts will increase what you receive back (on a vibrational level). On first thought this may sound great and too good to be true. But, there is a flaw, and many people overlook this important part. If you want to attract good, positive things into your business, then you can't simply think happy thoughts and expect it to happen. Just sitting at home saying "I want more money, I want fulfilment, I want recognition" (want statements) isn't going to create any of those things. So, do not expect a miracle to happen if you're not doing anything about it.

The key component, in my World, which is often crucially missed is "massive action." While having a good intention is respectable and needed, doing so without taking massive action will simply not bring about the results that you want. Successful entrepreneurs understand the value of taking action and nurturing their business. They take action consistently, and in doing this experience near vertical growth patterns. Simplifying this further, the more you do, the more you get.

ASK YOURSELF

 What "want statements" do you use daily that can be changed to "action statements"?

So using the above "want statements" as an example, you should aim to change your wants into "action statements". Such as: "What can I do to get more money?"or "What can I do to get more fulfilment?" or "What can I do to get more recognition?" Simply changing the way in which you ask the question radically changes the thought process and the results which appear. Massive action doesn't have to be as expensive as many business owners would assume and the majority of the time businesses already have the resources required. To start with *massive action* can involve anything from setting a new marketing strategy to building an affiliate scheme. Although these actions may not benefit your business within the next 5-10 hours; if you continue to do so on a daily basis it's not long before you'll start to the see the results.

Taking positive action is crucial to any business development. Unfortunately there are going to be times within the growth of your business, that success can seem very distant, perhaps unachievable. In times like these you should understand that as the probability law states, the more times you attempt a particular task the more chance you have of actually achieving that outcome. There is another simple but effective attitude change that will need to happen. In my World, the entrepreneurs who are the most successful are the very ones who are not afraid to fail over and over again. In fact many of my clients have changed the word failure to feedback, deleting the word entirely from their vocabulary. *Think about it* for a moment, if you could never fail at anything what more would you do?

TOP TIPS

- Schedule in 1 hour every day to take massive action within your business.
- Spend time outside of your business and look in objectively. Make small adjustments if you need to and then continue.
- Change the word failure to feedback in your vocabulary.
- Learn from your mistakes and accept feedback with open arms.

I believe that you can never fail at anything especially when you receive feedback; as you should look at feedback as a tool for development. It might be worth accepting that feedback is going to be part of your success. If something doesn't work then have another go by re-adjusting and learning what didn't work the first time. Remember, it is said that Thomas Edison took over 10,000 attempts to invent the light bulb, each time making small adjustments until he achieved his goal.

ASK YOURSELF

- How long would it take you to e-mail out an offer of 10% discount to all of your existing clients who buy within the next 48 hours? How much extra revenue would that generate for you this week?
- What more would you do if you couldn't fail but only received feedback?

Can You Deliver As An Entrepreneur?

During the last several years, I have met many admirable business owners all around the world with a dream of becoming the next Sir Richard Branson, Donald Trump or Anita Roddick. But unfortunately many of these people are doomed for failure! And the reason is simple:

As much as I support visualization within business, all too often these fluffy aspirations are influenced by late-night TV commercials, Internet get quick rich ploy's or heard from a friend down the pub as the next revolutionary niche. These eager business owners naively set off all guns blazing, spending valuable savings and time on their exciting new venture only to give up several months later, blaming everyone else for their lack of success.

The first thing to accept about "business" success is that these marketing schemes simply do not exist, and if they do I haven't heard about a good one. They are designed by very clever marketeers selling the idea of an extravagant lifestyle that can be achieved with little or no effort and *conveniently* with very little "upfront" monetary input.

Let's face it, if it were that easy; everyone would be doing it including me! I can't think of anything better than sitting down on a perfect tropical beach with my children, sipping a pina colada and reading a novel. The truth is, in order to get close to the dream (and it is possible), you have to establish what is realistically needed as an entrepreneur at the beginning. Taking time out to understand what is required at this early stage gives you the option to accept whether this is the right choice for you.

> **FACT**
>
> The vast numbers of roses sold on Valentine's Day in the United States are imported, mostly from South America. Approximately 110 million roses will be sold and delivered within a 3-day time period.

CHAPTER 1 GETTING HONEST

> **"People with goals succeed because they know where they are going... It's as simple as that"**
>
> - Vince Lombardi

In my World, if you were a fly on the wall and could see the beginnings of any business venture, I am certain that you would see an entrepreneur working 80 hours a week. Working at the kitchen table late into the night, networking while their employees were sitting down to watch TV, and the other not so glamorous sides of entrepreneurialism. The riches come long after. Don't get me wrong, I believe that everybody has the makings of an entrepreneur; able to create their millions and so live a life of wealth, abundance and happiness. However before they do, they must understand what a true entrepreneur is and what is going to be expected of them; because it isn't all pink roses and parties. Firstly, you have to figure out whether or not you are cut out to be one and if you are prepared to commit and sacrifice a lot to get there.

ASK YOURSELF

→ Can you afford to survive for one year financially?

→ Do you have the support from loved ones and do they understand the pressures involved?

→ Do you have the time to commit to the project?

→ Do you have the self-motivation required to carry this through to the end?

→ What are the major risks involved with starting today and are you still happy to continue?

If you are setting up a new venture or re-establishing an existing one, I would recommend making a list of all the pros and cons. What it is going to cost, not financially, but mentally and physically? Work out what is important in your life and whether if asked to do so, would you give it up? Consider how you might deal with losing your freedom for a while and whether the end result would be worth it. On a personal note, if you are in a relationship work through this with them. Make sure that they are on your side as this will save a lot of upset later down the line.

Another tip is to avoid taking the title of a "business owner" within your ventures. Virtually anyone can say that they run their own business and with the power of the Internet you could do it before you finish this chapter. Call yourself an entrepreneur, as it is very different.

ASK YOURSELF

 Can you handle setbacks and feedback without taking it personally?

 Are you mentally flexible enough to deal with objective thinking?

 Can you see the future more clearly than the next ten minutes?

In my World, the difference is clear between the two. An entrepreneur can clearly picture a long-range outcome and have a specific plan to build their business. They have a creative passion, deep enthusiasm and the ability to weather any storms. Entrepreneurs are renowned for being exceptional doers. While others are merely thinking about developing a product, an entrepreneur is out building the product, testing the product, re-inventing and re-evaluating if need be. They want to work on their business rather than within their business. They take time out to think objectively about where they are going, looking outside in, as opposed to a business owner who looks from the inside out.

Entrepreneurs are also expert delegators. They know how to plan, how to create and how to visualize a future of success and prosperity. In other words, investing in themselves and others to ensure their future success, rather than chasing the quick buck. Although it can appear to be just semantics, the more you grow as an entrepreneur the more you will appreciate the title.

So, crunch time, are you really cut out to be an entrepreneur? You need to ask yourself: What makes you different? Please understand that if you are doubting yourself, then that's fine and perfectly normal. Not everyone is cut out to run their own business or sacrifice certain things. After all, if everyone ran their own business there would be no one to work within these businesses. Make sure that you are fully aware of the risks involved and are 100% certain that this is the right time.

Do You Know Your Market And Do They Know You?

One of the most commonly neglected areas in a small to medium sized business is the subject of market knowledge. As blunt as it may sound, in my World, if your business plan does not stipulate the specifics of your market, then you are preparing your business to fail from the start. Do not fall into this trap or believe that it's not important for your industry, because it is!

I know that market research is one of the "not so glamorous" areas of business; in fact I find this incredibly boring. However any business whether just starting or continuing to run, that fails to recognize the importance of investing time and effort in market research, is massively reducing their chances of success and potential future growth. Part of the long term effectiveness of any business can be attributed to allocating time and resources to investigate their market. By dedicating just a small amount of time at the beginning of any venture can potentially save a lot of money and embarrassment in the long term.

Imagine for a moment (and this does happen) creating a product and not having a market? If there isn't a market for your product or service then you must think carefully about investing time and especially money. Avoid taking a stab in the dark within business as massive disappointment and debt often follows shortly after. My tip is to allocate some time investigating your market and have fun with it. Create a visual image and a written profile of your average client. If you can, get others involved within this creative project. A more varied input can offer many spins on the potential marketing opportunities.

> **ASK YOURSELF**
>
> → How big is your market and what percent market share do you need?
>
> → Does your client have a need to repeat the purchase and what are the average time scales?
>
> → Can this business be a sustainable income for you based on your findings?

For example, let's say that the product you are selling is specifically geared towards women. Your research suggests women are twice more likely to buy your product than men. Don't stop at these generalized findings, dig deeper and explore the specifics. The more detailed your description, the better your understanding of who your clients are and most importantly how you can market to them. Keep going: Are they stay-at-home mothers? Working professionals? Are they single or married? Are these women attending college or have they gone into their retirement years?

By doing this level of research you will begin to fully understand your target market and refine your marketing plan further. By knowing the specific group of potential clients for your product or service, you can narrow the focus of your marketing campaigns to target those particular clients. If you lack the budget to conduct this research then why not use data already collected by industry leaders? When you think about the millions of pounds that these large organizations spend on advertisements each year, you can easily assume that their market research is reliable.

> **"** You, too, can determine what you want. You can decide on your major objectives, targets, aims, and destination. **"**
>
> - W. Clement Stone

CHAPTER 1 GETTING HONEST

The next question to consider is whether or not your market knows you? You should be very clear about your unique selling point (USP) and how it's going to help you stand out from the more established brands. When a market is saturated and a client is faced with more than one option, you must ask yourself: Why they should choose you? What do you have to offer?

> **ASK YOURSELF**
>
> How is your business going to be successful if your clients don't know who you are?

The most common method that businesses use to distinguish themselves from others is the use of a strong brand. Your brand can take many forms, including a name, sign, symbol, colour combination or slogan. The word brand began simply as a way to tell one person's cattle from another by means of a hot iron stamp. Keep your business branding simple, as some of the most effective brands are clean and are easily recognized from glance. Think for a moment about the brands you see on a daily basis. For example: "Ford", "Amazon", "HBO", "EBay" "Virgin" and "Tesco". Research suggests that the product or service that maintains the highest brand awareness compared to its competitors will usually get the most sales. This higher rate of brand awareness also serves as an all important economic moat that prevents competitors from gaining a greater market share and protects your future sustainability.

> **FACT**
>
> The YKK that you see on zippers stands for Yoshida Kogyo Kabushiki Kaisha which is the name of the founder of the zipper manufacturing company in Japan.

Within your chosen industry it is also important to become the "trusted consultant", the expert within your field, the doctor of your industry. Make sure that this is communicated within your brand identity. Clients always like doing business with businesses that are regarded as experts. An excellent way to achieve this is to include a picture of yourself within the marketing material. It doesn't matter if you're selling a product or service as explained in later chapters. This will contribute towards brand awareness as it shows the client who they are buying into. *"A picture paints a thousand words."*

ASK YOURSELF

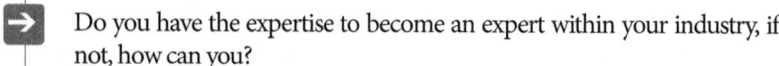
Do you have the expertise to become an expert within your industry, if not, how can you?

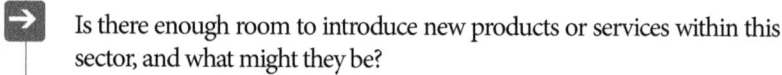
Is there enough room to introduce new products or services within this sector, and what might they be?

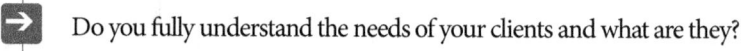
Do you fully understand the needs of your clients and what are they?

Knowing your market and ensuring they know you is definitely one of the hardest aspects of starting a new business. In an ideal World it would be great if every business succeeded simply by opening and inviting the media to the launch party. Unfortunately, this is rarely the case. Establishing brand identity and brand awareness takes time and often a lot of money, both of which are often in short supply when starting a business from scratch. In this sense it is important to spend your money wisely and make the right choice the first time.

In conclusion, incorporate brand awareness within your business and marketing plan from day one and do not forget it. This will address any issues that may arise when establishing who you are and what you are offering.

Is It The Best Business For You?

Too many business owners rush into business without knowing what they are good at. The next big tip is to make sure the business venture you do choose is the best for you. Take some time out to consider all of your options before committing to a particular business venture. If you already own a business and you're starting to question whether this is the best business for you, don't give up or jump ship as it's never too late to revamp your business and regain your enthusiasm. Taking the time now to reassess whether your business is actually the best business for you is essential; especially if you want the best chance of success.

When making this choice, you will need to do some self-realization and decide what your future may look like if you were to succeed. Is this really what you want and is it going to deliver what you think it will? If you need to, sleep on your decision, as you are more likely to make your choices based on facts as opposed to wild off-the-cuff aspirations.

A great way that you can do this is to have a full blown conversation with yourself in a mirror, discuss how this business fits in with your ideal life plan. Take notes of your thoughts to refer back to at a later date. This simple technique can uncover many different spins on your lifetime objectives and reveal the true purpose of your quest for excellence. If however you discover that you can't see yourself doing this particular business for the rest of your life then stop. Work out why and decide if you should continue to on this chosen path. If you can, and I would highly recommend it, spend some money on a professional therapist or business mentor, who can help you remove any preconceived notions or negative beliefs that may have been discovered during this exercise. A good coach will work with you on your possibilities and the elements of success that you already possess; identifying them and building them into your vision of the future.

FACT

 Microsoft made $16,005 in revenue in its first year of operation

During the early stages of any business it goes without saying that you are going to need to be completely focused. Any negativity you have will eat away at your motivation and later will create stress and self doubt. It is important that you overcome these issues early on as the quality of the internal relationship that you build could be the deciding factor on the level of success.

The more obstacles, the more resistance you will incur which will restrict the speed in which you achieve your outcome.

Something else to consider before making your choice, and as any successful entrepreneur will explain, you are likely to spend more time working on your business for the first several years than you will spend with your friends and family. You must ensure that you are really going to enjoy it and that you are receiving enough support from those closest to you in the process. It is also proven that when you enjoy doing something you also get a sense of fulfilment and therefore develop a positive attitude towards that particular task. Without it your work will quickly become a bore and the pressure of your social life will dominate your focus.

ASK YOURSELF

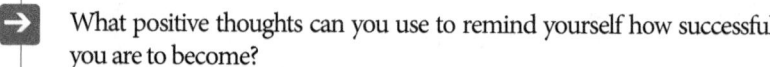 What positive thoughts can you use to remind yourself how successful you are to become?

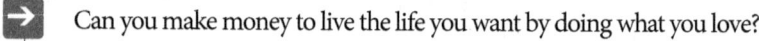 Can you make money to live the life you want by doing what you love?

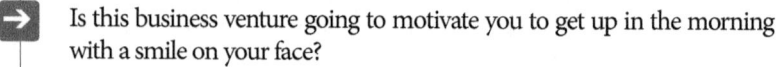 Is this business venture going to motivate you to get up in the morning with a smile on your face?

Once you are fully committed to your business venture it's important to maintain your enthusiasm. Avoid doubting yourself or putting limitations on what you can or cannot achieve. If you need a daily booster then remind yourself about those who had nothing and what they did to overcome their obstacles. There are a number of ways that you can do this including utilizing motivational quotes, visualisation exercises and vision boards. Whatever way you choose make sure that you practice this daily, as this can instantly change your mental state. If you start by putting limitations on what you believe you can achieve, then it is extremely unlikely that you will achieve even the smallest of the goals that you have set for your business, and soon lose the motivation to excel within that venture.

What Do You Personally Have To Offer?

When you have thought about the kind of business that you want and you're certain that it's the best choice for you, you then need to understand exactly what you personally have to offer, and how to overcome any weaknesses you may have. It is important to accept that if you are not 100% positively focused and confident in your own abilities; then you will not personally give your business the attention it deserves.

From first impressions the majority of entrepreneurs seem reserved about their ambitiousness and even at times play down their enthusiasm, but appear very self-confident and extremely knowledgeable. Although for less confident business owners this may seem like a facade, this self belief is simply because they know their personal boundaries. They channel their drive and determination into doing what they know they are good at, and are especially honest about what they are not.

Knowing what you personally have to offer your business is very important. Ultimately the internal projection (image) will create the beliefs about your abilities to achieve, and the image you project externally will create your perceived perception of how clients see you. A great exercise you can do to work this out is to go through your phone book and think about the friends that you would contact, and why, for any of the following suggested situations.

Who would you call if you needed money? Who would you call if you needed business advice? Who would you call if you needed directions? Who would you call if you needed relationship advice?

> ❝ The indispensable first step to getting the things you want out of life is this: decide what you want. ❞
>
> - Ben Stein

Now reverse this and think about what you have to offer and why those friends would contact you. Are you resilient? Are you skilful? Do you listen? You get the idea. Once you have your list look at your business and see how your skills can be applied; and what areas within your business complement each other.

Another method you can use to discover what you personally have to offer is to sit down and start to detail all the skills and talents you have. Start by brainstorming a list of things that you know how to do even if they don't initially seem remotely related to business. Then create subcategories of what areas of business they can be utilized within. For example: if you are good at communicating, then you should be one of the main people involved with the public. If you are not and come across blunt or brash then you should be kept away from the public.

One of the most amazing things about completing this exercise is that entrepreneurs rarely realize how much knowledge/skill they actually have until they see it visually on a page. If you feel comfortable in doing so, I would recommend showing the list to a friend and ask them to question what you have written down.

ASK YOURSELF

 Why are you going to succeed when many others don't?

 Have you got that burning desire to have money, recognition and fulfilment and why?

 Are your talents strong enough to make your business a massive success?

 Are you going to be able to deal with success once you have it?

Avoid concealing your skills and abilities by feeling vain as it will never make you a success. Being an entrepreneur is about being moral, honest and in particular being able to uncover skills or talents in yourself and others. One of my principles has always been that my success cannot be attributed to me alone but is in fact an amalgamation of the efforts of myself and my team. In my World, no person alone has or achieves anything on their own. In this sense it is useful to note that uncovering the best in others can bring out the best in you.

Are You Strong Enough Mentally And Physically?

Something that is often overlooked by entrepreneurs when starting their own business is whether or not they are strong enough to be their own boss. There's no question that starting your own business and building it from the ground up is not an easy task. Without the mental and physical endurance required, many business owners fall short and find themselves going out of business almost as soon as they started.

It is inevitable that you will experience some form of mental stress during the running of your business. It is therefore vitally important to plan for this and work towards maintaining low stress levels at all times. High stress levels can be a contributing factor to high blood pressure and other health problems which will not help you or your business.

Have you considered what steps you are going to take to reduce a build up of stress? Where are you going to go when you need to "let off some steam?" and "How are you going to deal with pressure?" Having answers to these kinds of questions is the key to staying sane!

Mentally Prepared:

In my World, the mental endurance of an entrepreneur is necessary in order to achieve greatness. Having a physiological edge enables you to be consistent, confident, focused, and determined during high pressure situations where others less able within these areas would crumble.

Studies have shown that spending a few minutes every day doing simple mind puzzles, playing games or simply learning a new language can build neural networks in the brain. Also it's suggested that there is an association between keeping cognitively active (playing games, solving puzzles) and a decreased risk of Alzheimer's disease. Take action before it becomes a need!

> **TOP TIPS**
>
> → Exercise regularly and have a hobby that takes your mind off your business.
>
> → Mini breaks/holidays, make sure that these are all unrelated to work!
>
> → Talk to friends and family about your problems and let them help. Keep a personal diary and write down how you feel.
>
> → Practice being calm, take time out to breathe or even meditate.

A common complaint amongst business owners is mental exhaustion; which is said to be a leading factor within depression. When times get tough in business it's evitable that it's going to have an effect on how you operate. Depression affects memory and effectiveness; even though it's a mental issue it can cause many physical illnesses. However it doesn't need to be; if you take preventative measures to control your physiology. You can relax, focus, and improve your chances of resolving any mental issues on identifying them.

Physically Prepared:

It goes without saying that keeping fit is a must within business; regular exercise can help you to reduce your risk of developing many health-related problems. For example: exercise can combat obesity, improve your circulation, and it can help prevent serious conditions such as heart attack and stroke. Exercise also triggers the release of a brain chemical called serotonin, which boosts your mood, and reduces feelings of anxiety and depression.

Exercise also tends to make a person more stable mentally, decreasing or eliminating major mood swings. Exercise reduces body fat and improves the physical appearance of people, which also improves self-confidence and mental attitude.

> **TOP TIP**
>
>
>
> You should aim to do a minimum of 30 minutes of moderate intensity exercise on at least five days a week. This can be done in one session, or it can be split into a number of sessions to work around your busy schedule.

In a recent study, young male and female volunteers were tested for "mood" and completed aerobics for just one hour. Of the 80 volunteers, 52 were diagnosed with depression before the exercise. After the workout they all reported a reduction in anger, fatigue, and tension. They also felt more energized. Exercise is proven to reduce anxiety for several hours afterwards.

Successful entrepreneurs know the importance of obtaining the correct mental and physical ability. Therefore I would recommend that you rule out time in your diary to take exercise; the more you do it the easier and more enjoyable it will become.

Why Is Now The Right Time?

A lot of people ask themselves whether now is the right time to start their business venture or not. For "unlucky" people the answer will always be "No". However, for entrepreneurs this answer will always be "Yes!"

Entrepreneurs accept there will never be a right time to start a business! In other words, the stars and planets will never align perfectly in such a way as to give you one clear signal that it's time to start your own business. They know that they would waste time fabricating many excuses and often remain at the planning stages waiting for the perfect day.

It is obvious that you will have to complete your due diligence, assess your market and put some financial stability to the side. But if you are honest there should really be nothing stopping you from beginning your journey into entrepreneurialism. Too many people look back at their life and say the dreaded words "What if?" Ask yourself now: Do you want to be that person?

If you doubting whether "now" is the right time to start your business then, get a pen and paper and start writing out when would be the right time. Once you have completed this go back and ask yourself whether this time is likely to ever exist; and when in the future that may be? At least by doing this when that time arises you will have already established why that time is the best, and you're unlikely to fabricate further excuses.

Once you are working within your business, procrastination can arise from time to time. Here are a few tips to avoid procrastinating within your business venture:

Make action statements:

Create action statements when you're studying any type of information, especially when looking to implement them within your business. Make sure they always produce a massive action as a result. For example "I should complete that task today." to "If I complete this task today, what can I do tomorrow to create more business opportunities?"

Get rid of fear:

Part of the reason we procrastinate is because we're afraid of what's going to happen when we get into the World of business. If you need to, seek guidance from professional coaches. You must actively take massive action to resolve these "learnt" fears.

Turn off distractions:

Keep any distractions away from your daily working; make sure that temptation isn't an option while you're being productive. Just because you have completed the one major task of the day, isn't an excuse to do something less productive. Tomorrow shouldn't be your solution to avoiding tasks.

Daily plan:

Spend 5 minutes scheduling your work for the next day. Allocate specific times within your diary and keep to them, break them down into micro tasks if you need to. However make sure they get completed before leaving for the day.

Do the most profitable activities first:

What is the most profitable activity in your business? Make sure that you prioritize the most profitable tasks first before moving onto those less profitable. Cleaning cups and hovering the carpet isn't going to increase your revenue, while calling potential clients is.

Reward yourself:

Set milestones and reward yourself accordingly. Once you have completed your daily tasks, get out and do something fun. Go to the driving range, perhaps go to the gym or meet a friend for coffee.

Accountability:

Make yourself accountable to someone for what you want to accomplish. This could be a business coach you work with or it could simply be a friend. They tell you their weekly goals and you tell them yours. Compare your goals and your results at the end of the week.

While on the subject of time, it is important to accept that becoming a successful entrepreneur rarely happens overnight. Avoid putting unnecessary pressure on yourself to achieve the now fashionable "celebrity status". Although it may seem that entrepreneurs achieve wealth and success overnight it is often forgotten that, prior to being in the public eye or limelight, the majority of them have actually dedicated years to developing their business empire. There is no rush, so enjoy the journey!

Remember: the final business masterpiece is likely to be the result of years of tiny "brushstrokes". Those moments of productivity that seem like nothing at the time, always build up to something big.

2 - Getting Started

2 Getting Started

Forget A Business Plan - A Cigarette Packet Is Good Enough!

Before setting up your own business, you will obviously need to think about writing a full business plan. This may seem like a monumental task to most, but you will be relieved to know that it doesn't need to be. If you're starting a new business venture, do not fall into the trap of believing that a business plan is something that you only need to write when requesting a loan from a bank! In my World, no business plan equals no business.

> "Our attitudes control our lives. Attitudes are a secret power working 24 hours a day, for good or bad. It is of paramount importance that we know how to harness and control this great force."
>
> - Tom Blandi

Think about your business plan as your business map, with success being the destination! If you are fearful of the business jargon associated with business planning then don't be. The majority of successful entrepreneurs who pursue more than one business venture, are generally more creative minded than they are business minded. Most budding entrepreneurs do not want to spend their time sitting down and drawing up a 50 page business plan prior to getting started. In fact, some of the best examples I have seen over the years have been written on a single piece of paper during a lunch break.

A good place to start is to describe your vision, detailing what it is that "you" actually want. How are you going to achieve it and within what time scales?

What outcomes you can expect? Describe the reasons why this business is best for you. Include information about who your clients are, and what your role is within the business. It should be noted that when it comes to writing a first-class business plan it's the quality that counts, not the quantity. Avoid the tendency to waffle, keep it clear and simple. A well-drafted business plan that covers all the key points has often proven to be worth its weight in gold; as certain business models can be duplicated if you choose to pursue another business venture.

> **FACT**
>
> Coupons were introduced in 1894 when Asa Candler bought the Coca-Cola formula for $2,300 and gave people coupons that he had written out to receive a free glass of coke.

If your business plan is to be used to request a loan to fund your business; your business plan will need to incorporate additional factual data such as cash flow worksheets, income projection and a breakdown of costs. You will also need to present a compelling argument for borrowing and a detailed report outlining ways in which you aim to pay the money back. It is also highly recommended to cover what will happen in the event of the expected sales not being met. For example: What securities have you that can be offered in the event of you not being able to pay your debt such as a house or savings?

If your business is not going to be funded by a benefactor, then a very simple business plan can be all that you need. Make sure you include goals and benchmarks that will summarize how exactly you will get your business from point A to point B. In this case, writing up something very simple to get you started is sufficient.

In a nutshell, a business plan can be viewed as a more detailed version of brainstorming. Within a business plan you simply write down your goals that will later help guide you to achieving your mission statement. If starting your business from scratch, then it's unlikely you will have information on financial areas so don't worry. It is therefore recommended to project what you expect to earn and how you estimated these figures.

> **ASK YOURSELF**
>
> → What information would you expect to see if you were lending money to someone?
>
> → How long would you lend them money before needing it back?
>
> → How would you incorporate this into your business plan?
>
> → How would you measure the risk of a business if viewing it from a third party?

A top tip at this stage is to create a business "income forecast sheet"; irrelevant of whether you're borrowing money or not. It's a useful tool which sets out when you will be able to start drawing money from your business. Do not fall into the trap of believing that you're going to be able to draw out a salary on day one; as it may be many months, perhaps years before you see a viable income. Examples of these can be downloaded off the Internet.

> **TOP TIPS**
>
> → Keep to the facts within your business plan. Give examples and more importantly include proof.
>
> → Write the business plan with success in mind. Ensure that you use positive language throughout.

While it is beneficial to have written a business plan for the obvious reasons, it is also important not to waste large amounts of time composing the perfect business plan. In truth, good business plans can be written within a few hours! A business plan is a great roadmap in getting you started. However the business plan itself is not going to earn an income or create success for you. It's the massive action you take afterwards that produces results. Successful entrepreneurs do not get caught up spending months in the planning stages of a business venture. They focus on the massive action established within the planning.

It's proven that getting started on your business plan can be the hardest point. I find the best way to start is to schedule in some time away from your business and get writing. Once started, avoid any interruptions and don't stop until you have all your ideas written down. Unlike school, this won't be graded on your first submission so don't be afraid to make a mess! Remember no business plan equals no business. Therefore, don't start your business venture without any written plan or forethought.

Here are a few basic tips for writing a business plan:

Come up with your business name:

The right name can make your business the talk of the town; the wrong one can doom it to obscurity and failure. So make sure you choose wisely. For example, avoid words that have negative connotations as you don't want to associate these with your business. Ensure you put as much effort into coming up with your business name as you did writing your business plan or even coming up with the business idea in the first place. Some business owners worry about what makes a good name. But in truth, any type of name can be effective providing it's backed by the appropriate marketing strategy.

Here are some methods successful businesses have used:

- ✓ Describe what you do. (Pets at Home, Easy Jet, Auto Trader)
- ✓ Abstract, random names that have nothing to do with your business. (Apple, Orange, Amazon, Virgin)
- ✓ Use your personal name. (Morrison's, McDonald's, Twinning's)
- ✓ Coined, made-up names (eBay, Tesco, Sony)
- ✓ Abbreviated names (HSBC, NHS, HBO)

Create a legacy statement:

Although often referred to as a mission statement, and explained in more detail later, a legacy statement clearly defines the essence or purpose of a business. Personally, I prefer to choose the word legacy over mission because a mission can eventually be achieved and therefore comes to an end. Whereas a legacy can live on forever. An effective legacy statement should be concise enough for you to describe your business's purpose and ideals in less than 30 seconds. Short and punchy is the key. The Coca-Cola company have several short legacy statements: To refresh the world... To inspire moments of optimism and happiness... To create value and make a difference.

See your vision:

It is important when coming up with a business vision to use your imagination. What vision do you have for your business 2 years from now? What about 5 years from now? Do you want to hire staff? Who are your clients? How will they find your business? Who is already achieving what you want on an international level? How can you achieve what they are and make it better? When do you want to sell your business or pass it down? Always start your business with the end in mind (exit strategy) and include these details within your business plan.

Create achievable goals:

What are the goals for your business? Make sure your goals are what are known as S.M.A.R.T. In other words: specific, measurable, attainable, realistic and timely. Don't be vague. Make them clear and specific; remember your mind only works towards the specifics that you give it. An example of a smart goal is "We will have £300,000 in retail sales of Product A&B by December 31, 20XX by doing XYZ. I can start tomorrow at 10.00am by calling the manufacturers with an order for ABC."

Put together a financial plan:

This potentially, can be one of the most difficult areas for a budding entrepreneur to grasp. Broadly speaking, a financial plan is a written strategy for spending and reinvesting future income. The financial plan states how the projected income will be allocated to various types of expenses, such as rent or utilities. It can also serve as an investment plan, stating how much is to be allocated to various assets or projects expected to produce further income, such as a new business or product line. Ask yourself, what are going to be your out goings/expenses and how much do you plan to reinvest in the future?

> **"We must walk consciously only part way toward our goal and then leap in the dark to our success"**
>
> - Henry David Thoreau

Weaknesses, Strengths, Opportunities:

It is important to be very mindful about being realistic when describing your strengths and particularly your weaknesses. It's natural to shy away from potentially critical weaknesses that you might not want to admit. But you must be honest with yourself! These underlying weaknesses need to be highlighted so that you can be aware of them. Only once they are highlighted can you improve or even eliminate them from the future.

ASK YOURSELF

- What industry developments can you foresee?
- How can you ensure that you hear about them first?
- Are there any industry changes arising that you need to be prepared for?
- Are you positioned correctly to compete with your competition?
- How will they react when you join the market?

At this point it is also worth considering what other opportunities you may want to pursue within your industry and when you will have the resources to do so. You need to be aware that your industry will never stay the same forever. You are going to need to expand and develop in-line with your industry, and so include your ideas and predictions within your business plan.

Once you have created your business plan and it has served its purpose of organizing you within the early stages of setting up your business; then what next? Many business owners incorrectly believe that a business plan is only useful when initially starting a business, but serial entrepreneurs know that the role of a business plan is to constantly assist and guide them. Get into the mindset of treating your business plan like your bible, your complete instruction manual. Include everything that would support another if they were left to run your business.

> "Do not wait for a change of environment before you act; get a change of environment by action"
>
> - Wallace D. Wattles

One of the main reasons for constantly updating your business plan is the market is constantly changing and this fundamentally effects how you go about your business. Subsequently, your business plan should always reflect growing trends within the market; and what you are doing to capture these opportunities.

How Big Is Big? – Conquering The World!

When starting a business, it is important to look beyond your actual market and niche area of interest from the very beginning. You should consider and visualise the bigger picture no matter how adventurous it may seem. Many business owners unnecessarily restrict the growth of their empire for no reason apart from only thinking about completing one task at a time and the short term goals. By this I mean that they only look for growth once their business is well established and the cash flow is looking good. In my World, this isn't the only time you should be thinking about the future of your business. Think of it like this, when you become "comfortable," it's likely that you will fabricate more excuses not to do something, due to a sense of contentment. You have done all the hard work, taken all the risks and now you want to sit back and enjoy it. Although this may sound like the sensible option, the problem is that once you stop a ball from motion you will always need a bigger force to get it going again.

> **FACT**
>
> According to research, the most productive workday is Tuesday and the least productive is Friday.

My theory is that it's much easier to continue moving forward once you are moving; the expansion of your business should not stop until you have achieved your legacy statement.

So again, how big is big? For some, big may be being the most successful person within a geographical area, but for many successful entrepreneurs it's much bigger. You should set the gauge based on how big your empire is to become. Not by its constraints such as: industry client base or the geographical location of your business; but by what you believe is the right limit for you.

Ask yourself this: Are you planning to work in your own local area or work internationally utilizing the vast resources of the Internet? Do you want global clients or local clients? Do you want one independent shop or a chain of stores?

If you are looking at the much bigger picture, then why not start by thinking about offering your products or services to a global market? Many business owners believe, often incorrectly, that they have nothing to offer the mass global market; but in my World, every business that clearly establishes a demand and a need within a market has something to offer the global community. It is simply a matter of repackaging or readapting to suit the types of client and the niches available on a larger scale. My father said to me once: "If you have something to sell to one; then why not sell it to many?"

> **ASK YOURSELF**
>
> If your business could be the biggest it could be, how big would it be?
>
> Are you thinking locally or globally?

For example: If you are a plumber, your skill is primarily "knowledge"! As a plumber, it would be counter-productive for you to jump on a plane and head to Brazil to fix a toilet! Generally a plumber's target market is based within a 100 mile radius of their office. However, as discussed later in more detail, there are global opportunities for almost every business owner who aims to branch out, including skilled professionals. A plumber, by selling and packaging their skill, could set up an online training business that would demonstrate how to conduct basic home plumbing; or perhaps an online parts store selling at wholesale prices. The plumber could even consider setting up a branded fleet of franchisees within their district.

The opportunities for any business are endless; it is only restricted by the restraints imposed by their legacy statement.

"The sky is your limit, it depends how far you want to reach."

If you are thinking about investing in global trading in the future, then it is essential that you include this within your initial business plan. Start with compiling a local plan followed by a national plan, and then an international plan. Ensure that you clearly differentiate between the three so that if one reaches a hurdle or delay, then the other two don't suffer.

Doing this now gives you the option to change your mind in the future. If you did later change your mind and you failed to build this into you business plan at the beginning; your business may require major reconstruction to adapt to the global market. Thus incurring significant costs and disruption.

> **FACT**
>
> The average number of pillowcases washed a day at the MGM Grand Hotel in Las Vegas is 15,000.

Thinking globally changes the thought planning process, requiring you to consider the steps you should be making to ensure that your products and services are potentially available to everyone. Spend time during this planning process developing these ideas, as they could determine the vehicles (such as newspaper, posters, TV, website) you would use to advertise. For example you might avoid choosing a local newspaper to advertise your product as the audience size is relatively small to that of the Internet. If you're planning to "go global" then think big in everything you do.

" The most important thing about goals is having one "

- Geoffry F. Abert

If you have decided that you want to take the big jump and aim big, but not sure where to start, then e-commerce websites are excellent platforms on which to sell products to a global market. E-commerce websites have radically changed the way that smaller business can operate and the reason for the phenomenon known as globalization. If your business is based on products, then you should already without a doubt be utilizing the Internet (e-commerce website) to globalize your business. If you already have a website but do not have this option, then this can be done by contacting your web developers (or the person who created your website). Inquire whether it is possible to incorporate a products section and a shopping cart within the functionality. Before you start you should research whether or not the item can be shipped to certain countries, as there are laws and regulations related to certain products including import and export taxes.

Here are a few things to consider when exploring global trade:

Time:

You will be called upon and expected to respond to customer service issues at any time, all of the time. Make sure that you incorporate this within your global planning. Display clearly on your website time zone and the working hours of customer service. If you have the need, consider outsourcing the customer services to call centres experienced within your sector.

Language:

Remember that not everyone speaks or understands English. Although it is considered to be the predominant language used on the Internet, it may produce limitations on the country and your target market. If your target market requires an alternative language, ask your web team to clone your current website and have the content translated.

Monetary conversion:

Decide what currencies that you offer/can offer. There are many programmes available online that offer simple to use conversion tools. When building your e-commerce website ensure that this is a consideration and how it can be incorporated.

Appropriateness:

You must decide whether the foreign market is really a good market for you. Does your sense of style or business come across appropriately to your foreign visitor? Do you have the right product or service for a foreign market?

Regionalisms:

Make sure that you have someone with an understanding of International Language to proof your website content. Certain words do not translate appropriately to other similar speaking countries, and you will not want to use language that could be seen as offensive.

Cost:

Make sure that you are fully aware of all of the costs involved with exporting goods from your country to the next. Remember to include taxes, delivery costs, return costs and so on. Falling to build these within your planning could be an expensive mistake.

The Internet provides opportunities for international exposure and business transactions never before dreamed of, but don't be lulled into thinking it'll be easy or quick. This exercise can be costly during the initial stages but can be massively rewarding if you plan carefully.

Get The Professionals Behind You – The Extra Crutch

In my World, there is no doubt that behind every successful entrepreneur there is guaranteed to be a team of professional consultants advising and recommending the best choices for the growth of their business. I have them within my business and would recommend that you have them within yours.

Successful entrepreneurship is primarily about identifying a need and providing an effective solution, but this is a an area that can often be overlooked within your own business. By this I mean it is near on impossible to do everything in your business and be 100% effective, even if you wanted to. As your business grows and your time becomes more valuable, you are going to need the advice of various trusted professionals or at least have the knowledge of who they are.

Successful business ownership is about knowing when to ask for help, who to have on your team and when the time is right to delegate. Over the years I have seen many unfortunate business owners fail to make it through the second year of trading simply because they are trying to do too many things at once.

My theory is simple and it overcomes any potential competency issues. If you can't perform the task more efficiently or effectively than someone else; then outsource the job right from the beginning. I don't understand why any business owner would slave over completing their tax return and accounts, flyer design or even researching legalities. When for less money in time and effort they could have hired a professional to complete the task for them. In my World, all entrepreneurs should always work with the "law of least effort," meaning that your time and efforts are always going to be better spent creating and developing new innovative ideas. Do not worry about how you can save the £10.00 on your insurance renewal, or spend hours designing and deciding what banner design looks best for your affiliate scheme.

TOP TIPS

 Create a culture within your business. Some of the best companies I have worked with have cultures that are "rigorous but not ruthless."

 Whenever you have a task to complete, ask yourself: Are you the best person to complete this task? What could you do to move your business forward if you commissioned someone else to do it?

Here are a few types of professionals you may need to drive your business forward:

An Accountant:

Avoid judging the value of an accountant on how much they charge annually; but instead on the amount of money they could potentially save you within your business lifetime. Their role is to guide and advise you on how to make the most from your money. If you can, ask them for an annual fee, which often includes a service that allows you to call them at any time (within business hours) with questions regarding monetary issues. This will avoid consultant fees and extra charges. Don't be afraid to ask lots of questions as these people are there to help.

A Lawyer:

It's inevitable within your business life that you will require the services of a legal professional. Save time by choosing a lawyer at the beginning, as this will avoid delays when you really need one. You don't want to lose a contract because you're wasting precious time looking for a suitable lawyer who has expertise in your particular field of industry. Outsource 100% of your debt chasing to your legal professionals. Ask them for a letter by letter cost and how much commission they claim from all successfully received funds.

Business Mentor/Coach:

Over the last several years, countless people across the globe have undergone some form of mentoring programme and now are branding themselves as some form of industry expert. Although these so-called business mentors mean well, I would recommend working with someone who has experience within your industry and who can show you a proven business portfolio. The main role of a business mentor is to add accountability to your goals and answer any business related questions you may have. Remember seeking advice isn't a weakness but a highly effective skill.

An Insurance Broker:

An insurance broker acts as an intermediary between you and insurance companies. Insurance brokers work to ensure that you are suitably insured to practice and operate within your industry. Avoid buying an insurance scheme based on cost opposed to cover. If you have expensive, high tech equipment and your business cannot function without it; make sure that it is included within your cover and that it is a like for like policy (replaced to specification and not to value). Also discuss repair or replacement options with the broker to ensure your business is not at risk in the unlikely event of fire or theft.

Graphic/Web Designer and Marketing Team:

With the World constantly evolving around the Internet and online shopping, it's very important to keep up with the times and make sure that you are as equally presented as you are enthusiastic. Build a good relationship with a design team and get them to design all of your marketing material. Avoid jumping from one to another as there will need to be consistency across all of your work. Make sure that you provide them with all the information about your plans for the future as this may have an effect on the style and type of designs they create.

Bank Manager:

Make sure that you "hire" a bank manager that understands the needs and objectives of your business. Don't be afraid to interview potential business account managers before making your final decision. Remember they work for you and not the other way around.

> **"This one step, choosing a goal and sticking to it, changes everything."**
>
> - Scott Reed

Having the support of other professionals who know your business inside out can often be the difference between a successful business and a total disaster. Work towards assembling a team that you can always count on to help you stay focused. Remember that your success should always be their success, and their success should always be yours.

If you are unsure as to where to find such trusted professionals, I would recommend getting involved in local networking groups. Here you may find the professionals themselves or often you will meet business owners who are able to recommend reliable professionals they have worked with in the past. These are not only great places to get more contacts, but are also places to "mingle" with other like-minded people, giving you an opportunity discuss business ideas and in some cases, receive advice or feedback from others with experience within the business industry. Remember every business owner started somewhere and generally will give advice freely when asked.

In summary, be very honest with yourself and make sure that you assess if you are the right person to take care of certain aspects of your business. If you know for a fact that you are terrible with your own bank account, then you do not want to place your business's banking needs in your own hands. Hire a bookkeeper for a couple of hours on a monthly basis who can handle those tasks. However, make sure you spend this saved time wisely on developing your business. Just because someone else is doing it for you, does not give you an excuse for some time off!

You Don't Need A Ferrari – What Are The Basics?

When starting your own business, it is very easy to get carried away and develop a big ego. After all, you can now call yourself a "Business Owner" or a "CEO". It is however, important to not let your ego get in your way. Most people associate business owners and CEO's with high incomes, but in reality, just because you can call yourself these things does not necessarily mean you are a millionaire (especially in the early stages). Spending your money intelligently is critical in the overall success or failure of your business.

> **ASK YOURSELF**
>
> → What do you really need for your business to function? A telephone, desk, computer, printer, fax machine?
>
> → How can you reduce the overheads for the first two years of your business?
>
> → How can this money saved be better invested?
>
> → What is the most effective way you can get your business started on a shoestring?

All too often newly appointed business owners get very excited when they receive the first profits, believing they have "made it", and so consequently don't think before they act. They rush out and rent luxurious office space with great views, buy a commercial lot, rent a pricey copier or purchase a prize vehicle to impress their clients or friends. They produce a facade of material objects that make people believe that their business is successful. But in reality they often don't have sufficient funds or the constant flow of profits to grow or develop, and so in the end become stagnant and close. Allowing your debts to uncontrollably build up is, in my opinion, where most businesses fall into the trap of "spiral debt"!

I personally do not think that there is anything wrong with wanting these luxuries for your business. But if you want to ensure later success and further profits you need to postpone buying these items until they are absolutely necessary and your business can really afford them! Reserve your profits (particularly your initial ones) and only reinvest in the areas of your business that are going to produce additional profits. This I'm afraid often rules out the more excitable, flashier luxuries! Don't let your ego bring down your business. Remember: expand in line with your cash flow and not in line with your borrowings.

> **FACT**
>
> In 1915 William Wrigley Jr. sent chewing gum to everyone in the phone book, targeting the wealthy households.

For instance, would it make more sense to spend £3000 either renting a luxurious office space or spending this on marketing? Whereas the office space offers a "wow factor" and so serves to boost your ego and impress your friends, it is unlikely you will gain any profit out of this. You are more likely however, to produce more profit in the long run by investing in things such as marketing new product lines. Think about it for a moment, who will see your fancy new office if you are not telling clients who you are and where you are by means of marketing?

When starting a business my tip is to: "go basic". Begin by writing a list of the essential tools you require to get started. If the great Henry Ford can start designing and building a car on his own farm and consequently built the famous Ford brand, then so can you. The theory is to start your business on a "shoestring" and assess your financial position as you move forward with profits. You should also think carefully about investing large amounts of your own money until you can clearly see the direction in which your business is moving. You don't want to liquidize your resources in an area only to learn later that it isn't what you like, isn't lucrative enough, or is not really your skill set.

> ### TOP TIPS
>
> If you are asking for a loan then ask for more than you need. This way you will have always a backup if your business meets a difficult hurdle.
>
> Make sure that the repayments are built into your business plan, don't forget to add the interest.

For example, let's say you start a consulting business called "Strategic Consulting", you begin by providing one-on-one management consulting sessions with CEO's and other business owners. Later however, you realize that your forte is really within the coaching and personal development field and change your name to "Strategic Thinking". You now need to spend money adapting your business to suit the new direction. If you have spent all your resources on the first direction (providing one-on-one management consulting sessions with CEO's and other business owners) how will you afford this new venture?

> **"He who has a why to live for can bear almost any how."**
>
> - Friedrich Nietzsche

Being clever with your money should be a must for you and the success of your business.

The Bank – Who's Got The Money?

Before starting your business, it is probable that you will need "ready" money. While some businesses only require £200 to set up, others may need £200,000 or in some cases even more. Unfortunately most entrepreneurs when starting out on a new business venture will not have access to this amount of cash, or have not come from a privileged background that can support them. In these cases you must pursue alternative financial avenues.

One of the most effective ways of securing this initial capital is by means of a business loan. A business loan is very similar to a personal loan but generally assessed on your business proposal rather than you; although personal considerations are also included. To secure a bank loan you will normally need to successfully pitch your business venture to the bank's business account manager. This is achieved with the use of a well comprised business plan; one that clearly demonstrates your goals, objectives, methods and loan details.

> **FACT**
>
> Fossilized bird droppings are one of the chief exports of Nauru, an island nation in the Western Pacific.

Although a misconception, banks are always looking for profitable opportunities to invest in, as they also need to keep in business! They can however be very "picky" when it comes to choosing which opportunities to accept and which to turn down, especially during times of economic downturn. It is worth noting that without a proven previous track record in business, securing a bank loan may be difficult. This means that you must build a solid case for borrowing and overcome any objections within your business.

From experience the first loan is usually the hardest to get, but once you are on the ladder it's plain sailing, as banks are far more likely to approve a loan for an established business or someone they consider a low risk over a start-up or emerging business. This is largely because banks work on a "risk" system. They need to be convinced that you are a reliable investment. They therefore prefer to lend money to borrowers who have borrowed at least once and have a good track record with borrowing and repayment. Remember that they are not the venture capitalists who make slightly higher-risk loans. Banks prefer (but don't always) to lend to low-risk ventures to ensure that they will see a return on their investment.

> **TOP TIP**
>
> The way to wealth lies first in eliminating debt, which lightens the spirit and makes you more confident and therefore more productive.

It is important to note that although banks do tend to go with the lower risk option, this is not to say that they never consider some higher risk ones as well. To overcome their fears they may decide to loan you the money but with certain conditions. These could include a higher interest rate or on a shorter term. For instance, you may be required to undergo a shorter three year repayment plan. This will give your business plenty of time to establish whether it is going to work, and the bank have an opportunity not only to receive the investment back but to judge the effectiveness of your business plan. It is therefore always essential to present your business venture as "low risk" when asking for money from a bank as you will avoid these measures that banks take to ensure they see a return.

Here are some steps that you should take to improve your chances of getting that first bank loan:

Double check that you have a solid personal credit rating:

The newer the business, the more closely the individual behind it will be evaluated. In order to prove that you are a "low risk" opportunity you need to make sure you get your own financial records in order before asking a bank for money to start a business. A solid personal credit rating is very important, since a small business is typically an extension of the individual who starts it. If you have had a good history of handling your personal finances, then the chances are that you will know how to protect and make a return on the bank's investment in your business.

> **There is one quality that one must possess to win, and that is definiteness of purpose, the knowledge of what one wants, and a burning desire to possess it.**
>
> - Napoleon Hill

If you don't have a good credit history then don't worry, be honest and explain anything that may arise before they check. Personally, even if you are sure that you have a solid credit rating, I would recommend registering with a credit referencing agency before asking for a loan. In most cases you can sign up for a free 30 day online trial. Double check to make sure all is in order as sometimes errors can occur or previous finance companies may forget to remove data. If all looks good then you can add this to your business plan. But if not, then you will need to resolve all of the issues before proceeding to a bank.

Be sure all your documents are neat, legible and organized in a cohesive manner:

Type all your loan documents. Handwritten documents tend to appear unprofessional. Make sure that your business plan is up-to-date, organized and well presented. Avoid dog-eared paper with coffee stains. The presentation of your business plan is indirectly a representation of you! You only get one chance to impress, so make this one count!

Be honest! Avoid stretching the truth:

You should also prepare financial statements for your business as you need to show them the current financial position of the business. Obviously if your business is brand new you will not have much information to show them. Here you will need to build projections based upon other similar businesses in your area and industry. But make sure that these businesses are still trading!

> **TOP TIPS**
>
> → Make sure your business plan is well presented and detailed.
>
> → Include your projections for up to three years with facts and evidence to support the projection.
>
> → Write a short biography about yourself and experience within this sector and what qualifies you as an industry expert.
>
> → Include references. If you know successful business owners include them, the banks generally like name dropping.

Be honest, it is likely that the bank manager will have had some experience with others in the same industry. Do not bend the truth or expand the figures to look good. Broad, unsubstantiated statements must be avoided. The bank manager can easily check many of the facts in your business plan. So, if you cannot support statements with solid data, then don't make them. Do your homework and spend time doing research to be able to support everything you say, including every single number in your projections. I would recommend keeping projections, assets lists and collateral statements on the conservative side.

Be prepared and learn to anticipate every question the bank may ask:

Build a bullet proof case file, pre-empt any questions they may ask and prepare an answer backed with evidence. Always ask the bank prior to the meeting what they would like to see and what is their current lending criteria, as this may change from bank to bank. The more you are organized the more likely that you will receive the outcome that you want or very close to it. Remember, the combination of information and preparation is the most powerful negotiating tool in the World.

Choose the correct bank:

To increase your chances of getting a loan, it may be wise to consider carefully which banks you approach. You could start with banks that you have done business with in the past as they will be familiar with your previous financial behaviour and history, but it is also good to visit banks that you have no history with but are actively looking for more business. Scour the newspaper for banks that are advertising for more business. If this is your first loan request, then it is advised to look for a bank that is familiar with your industry and who has done business with companies like yours.

Don't avoid discussing risk within your business plan:

Banks understand that there is no business without an element of risk. If you do not discuss risk, the banks will assume that you haven't considered it. It is important to remember that entrepreneurs cannot plan for everything, for every contingency, for every turn of events. The bank will want to know if you have planned for the major risks and how you intend to keep these risks low.

For example: A risk that you may not have thought about is the risk of too much success! The demand for your products or service may exceed well beyond your expectations, and the bank would want to know how you intend to handle this success.

Keep approaching one lender after another until you get your loan:

If declined don't give up! Keep refining your business plan until a backer sees your business as a wise investment. Don't ask your friends and family for a loan even if they are in a financial situation to help, avoid this at all costs as this can create friction and in some cases destroy your relationship. Keep your business strictly professional and avoid personal ties if you can. However if you want them involved ask them to help in other ways. Before you decide to approach a bank directly, you could ask an associate, friend or acquaintance that is in good standing with the bank to give you a positive referral. From experience banks tend to deal more favourably with those who were referred to them by their best clients.

Peer-to-peer lending:

If you are slowly running out of options you could consider peer-to-peer lending. Peer-to-peer lending has only recently become popular and is offered by a select few online websites.

> **"Visualize this thing you want. See it, feel it, believe in it. Make your mental blueprint and begin."**
>
> - Robert Collier

The best way to describe peer-to-peer lending is that it is a type of auction. You list the kind of loan you require and potential investors "bid" on your post. You then choose to accept either the lender offering the lowest interest rate or generally the most suitable offer. Once accepted the money is deposited into your account and each month the payment is drafted automatically back to the investor who won the bid.

> **TOP TIP**
>
> Remember the saying "Without self-mastery you can never master others."

Before deciding how to fund your business venture ensure you look at all the options. If you need to consult your trusted consultant then do so, avoid picking or going with the first choice. Look at all options and choose the best based on your specific needs.

Get Educated – Learn The Mistakes Of Others By Reading Daily

One thing that I have learned in business is that learning never stops! Many business owners I meet have lost the skill of learning or believe that learning is a waste of time. They believe that just because they are in business that they possess the knowledge of how to "survive" in business, and they are probably right. However merely surviving isn't what all effective entrepreneurs want, in fact any business owner that wants to merely survive may just achieve that legacy. From my experience effective entrepreneurs want to build, develop and inspire others, and in order to do so they must learn.

> **FACT**
>
> In 2001, the five most valuable brand names in order were Coca-Cola, Microsoft, IBM, GE, and Nokia.

As I have mentioned throughout this book industries are always changing, and therefore you will also have to. All too often unsuccessful business owners are shocked to find that what they have learned in the past has become outdated and no longer applies to their current business. Learning can be the deciding factor between businesses that grow and those who stay stagnated and consequently lose motivation. Learning does not need to be difficult especially if the right techniques are implemented, and more importantly doesn't have to take time out of your schedule.

Think about the amount of time that you spend in your car on the way to work or travelling in general. Rather than listening to the latest music charts you could download business audio books and turn your car into a mobile university. Listening to motivational CDs and other audio books, lessons or seminars during your morning commute is an effective way to utilize this normally unproductive "spent" time. Audio books can massively assist in the development of your business and your career as well as your life. Just simply taking the time to listen to them before a sales presentation, interview, or business meeting, can radically change your way of thinking and the future results.

If you use public transport then you might want to invest in a portable device (MP3 player) that will still allow you to listen to your lessons as you travel. Feeding your subconscious mind with alternative information during this time spurs new ideas and alternative ways of thinking. This can provide different spins on the direction that you're taking within both your business and life.

> **Patience and perseverance have a magical effect before which difficulties disappear and obstacles vanish**
>
> - John Quincy Adams

In addition to listening to audio books I would also recommend registering with business related websites offering weekly articles. These can be a valuable resource of great ideas and articles written by industry experts. It's also a great way to learn about the mistakes that other businesses have made and how you can potentially avoid them. Within these articles you will often read about businesses that have failed or filed for bankruptcy, leaving gaps in the market for your potential growth. Learn from their mistakes. Remember the failure of others is your feedback. By dissecting other businesses you can make changes in your own to ensure you don't suffer the same fate.

Here are a few external focus points to get you started:

Internal driving forces:

Internal political events, corporate culture and sub-cultures, internal technological capacity, employee proficiency, efficiency, and productivity, financial stability, professional development, human resources, communications policies.

External driving force:

Political environment, economic environment, social and/or cultural environment, technological, environment, demographic changes, competition strategies and tactics.

In my World, life in general is about learning from our mistakes and the mistakes of others so that we can improve mentally and physically. By keeping up-to-date with the latest changes in your industry, you will always be on the cutting edge of what's hot and what's not.

> "Kites rise highest against the wind— not with it."
>
> - Winston Churchill

In summary, education in business is power. By knowing more you have the advantage of being flexible in times of need. My father quite rightly said: "If you're not learning you're dying."

Procrastinating Promise – The Best Time To Start Was Last Year

In my World, successful entrepreneurs should never procrastinate, as it kills the very ideas that make an entrepreneur successful.

Procrastination is a behaviour that every business owner will fall into at some stage through their career. Although it might appear that there is not a logical reason for procrastination. Human behaviour is not coincidental, for everything we do; there is a reason. In fact, everything we do, we do for a positive intent. Everything is driven by a desire to improve our circumstances at some level of our consciousness.

This is a very important concept to understand if you are to take preventative measures to ensure that this doesn't happen to you. Although there are many reasons on the surface as to why you procrastinate, the underlying reason will always come down to one major factor: FEAR. Fear is what shuts you down and prevents you from taking massive action.

> **ASK YOURSELF**
>
> Think about it for a moment, when was the last time that you didn't do something?
>
> Thinking back to it now, what was the reason?

Fear ultimately is there to "help" you as a human being. It's a natural instinct that protects you from potential harmful situations. By default the mind will always be compelled to prevent an encounter with it. Although fear is the underlying factor behind procrastination, there are certain common fears amongst procrastinators. Here are what I believe are the most common reasons for procrastination and the fears that we subconsciously attach to them:

The fear of failure:

When you fear failure you are inclined to avoid doing something in the first place and on most occasions avoid that topic all together. The common language used in this circumstance is that: "If I don't do it, then I can't fail and no one can judge me." This is very prominent amongst business owners as they often idealize perfection and protect themselves against anything that would jeopardize this happening. They will wait for things to be perfect until they take action, so they keep postponing tasks waiting for the 'right time' before they take action. Out of the fear of failing and looking bad, they will often spend vast amounts of time on a project without making any real progress because at a subconscious level they don't "want to" finish. A finished project will make them vulnerable for criticism and consequently failure.

The fear of painful experiences:

If you believe that some action will lead to a painful or unpleasant experience then you will feel compelled not to do it. Although that seems like a sensible attitude to have it isn't. Your nervous system is designed to avoid painful experiences. The ironic thing is that we get to decide what we believe, and what will be "painful" experiences.

> **TOP TIP**
>
> Before following the pattern of what you believe is a painful experience, ask yourself why it isn't?

Unfortunately for most of us, our beliefs were "installed" by default and we learned by association; usually when we were young. If you believe that some action will lead to a painful or unpleasant experience; you will avoid it, regardless of whether your association is accurate or not. What you believe is what's real for you and this is what you will act upon.

The fear of missing out:

In the frenzy of modern living we all want to get a piece of the action. We simply cannot help it. Every day we get bombarded with numerous opportunities and it seems like the media's sole mission is to get our attention. The challenge is that we don't want to miss out. No one wants to be left behind and miss out on what everybody else is gaining from. The challenge with this is that we tend to take on way too much, to the point where we get overwhelmed. When you feel overwhelmed, the natural reaction is to shut down and the result is usually procrastination. When you overload yourself with too many things that you "have to do" you simply cannot deal with all of it and procrastination comes to your "aid". Like a breaker switch in an electric current, procrastination will kick in when the load becomes too heavy.

These factors are by no means the only reasons for procrastination, but they are definitely some of the most common. An awareness of these fears in itself can help you to overcome procrastination. Realize that F.E.A.R is only an acronym for False Evidence Appearing Real and most of your fears are only imaginary. It is your conscious responsibility to direct and steer your life. Don't allow procrastination and indecision to keep you immobilized. Keep moving forward and keep taking *massive action*.

MAGIC FORMULA

Positive affirmations + Massive actions = Unbelievable results!

3 - Research Get On With It!

3 Research - Get On With It!

Tell Everyone! They Help You, You Help Yourself

When talking to business owners and discussing why tasks have been left unfinished, or even abandoned, many excuses are presented. However after more deeper questioning the root cause often comes down to the fact that they feel embarrassed to ask for help. This can be an unnecessary stumbling block for many business owners and here is why:

One thing that is very clear about all entrepreneurs, they by their very nature tend to be very proud of their unique way of thinking and abilities. They assume incorrectly, that others are unable to complete tasks to their own high standards or expectations. This assumption however can contribute to their downfall, particularly as they can restrict themselves, their opportunities and also waste essential time when they can simply "get on with it".

> **FACT**
>
> Close to fifty percent of Internet shoppers spend over five hours a week online.

It is imperative to accept early on that within your business venture you will at some stage require others to assist you on your path to success. Yes, you are going to have to ask for help! Successful entrepreneurs who run sustainable businesses agree that no matter how talented you may think you are, you will undoubtedly need help from time to time. Sadly, developing this attitude is often restricted by an individual's pride or in some cases their ego.

Consequently, being able to delegate, take a step back and so allow experts to be involved, is a skill that most entrepreneurs learn the hard way. Although a common misconception in society, asking for help doesn't make you weak or incapable of handling your own business affairs. In fact, recognizing the need for assistance is one of the most responsible actions that you can take for your business. Successful entrepreneurs often give the persona of a superhero, an "I can do anything" status. But in reality they will have received some guidance or assistance prior to their success.

In the beginning some entrepreneurs are reserved when it comes to discussing their new business venture with friends and family. These entrepreneurs want to avoid embarrassment and so hold back until their business is succeeding before they boast. However this can actually stunt the success of the business as family and friends are those who are ready without question to support and believe in you the most!

TOP TIPS

 Ask your friends and family to post adverts on their social media pages, such as Facebook, Twitter, YouTube, Linked In, or Orkut. (For a full list of social networking websites Google: social networking).

 Offer discounts or incentives to any leads that come through a referral, such as 10% off or a free product when mentioning their name or a unique code.

It is also important to note that collectively a friends and families social network is vast. By utilizing this network effectively you could potentially increase the number of people who are aware of your business. Begin by mentioning your business to those around you and you'll be surprised how quickly "word gets around". It is best to visualize this as an inverted pyramid, one person informs two people, and those two people inform three others and so on. You just need to start the "chain"!

An effective way to begin this "chain" is to design a simple e-mail/flyer offering a discount, exclusive to extended friends and family. It's a proven fact that clients prefer to buy from a familiar face, someone they know rather than a stranger. (Remember it helps if you include a picture of yourself within the marketing.) This type of viral marketing is very beneficial and could build your client base quickly and in particular produce pre-qualified leads fast. Pre-qualified leads save time and money as the client is already interested in your product/service.

> **FACT**
>
> Every year, kids in North America spend close to half a billion dollars on chewing gum.

I understand that entrepreneurs feel apprehensive when asking friends and family to assist them with marketing. But if you think about it, is one of the most logical steps to take. Start with the people closest to you and work outwards to those who you know the least. Once some have started to help you'll notice how others seem to want to help you.

Marketing is obviously critical to any business, but unfortunately is often ignored until later within the business lifetime. While I do agree that it is unwise to mix personal life with business, at certain times you should not completely conceal your business intentions from those closest to you. They can offer a very affordable option to marketing your business which is particularly essential within the first stages of business.

Outside the network of your friends and family, another way to build a client database and receive pre-qualified leads, is to attend and get involved with business networking groups. A business networking group is simply a group of like-minded people that typically meet 2 to 4 times per month, all with intentions of generating new business leads. Each networking group may work a little differently, but the basic concept is always the same. During these networking events each business owner or representative acts as an extended sales force to the other businesses within the group; offering potential prospects and leads to others who have attended the meeting. The idea is simply to general more business for others within the group.

Before you consider attending a networking group it is important that you are appropriately prepared. With a powerful pitch and presentation you can make a positive impact with the people that you meet during these events; without one you will get lost in the hustle and bustle of those more able networking gurus.

In order to be prepared, spend some time in advance creating a short "elevator pitch" describing your business. This should be a short 15 to 30 second speech that is quick, to the point and punchy. Avoid long and "boring" pitches where your audience has the opportunity to lose interest.

> " I do not think there is any other quality so essential to success of any kind as the quality of perseverance. It overcomes almost everything, even nature. "
>
> - John D. Rockefeller

Make sure that your elevator speech creates a positive impact and differentiates you from competitors within your industry. If you are a small business consultant, unknown outside your industry sector, then you might want to create a statement explaining what makes you successful and unique within your industry.

For example instead of saying: "I'm a small business consultant looking for business." you could say something more specific like: "I recently helped the multi-national company John Smith Manufactures decrease their marketing costs by 50% and increase profit by a whopping 30%, I am looking to help like-minded professionals save money." Once you have created your elevator speech, read it out loud so that it is easier for you to ensure that the speech makes sense and isn't too forward.

Another affordable way to build up your client base with pre-qualified clients is by third party referrals. These clients approach you after receiving a recommendation by a friend or associate. You need to remember that business owners don't just talk about their own business; they also discuss other businesses too, especially if they have a personal gain. Make sure that it is your business they are recommending. You can achieve this easily by doing the same for them or offering incentives for any leads they pass through.

> **TOP TIPS**
>
> → Create a list of ways your product and services can help clients based on facts and testimonials.
>
> → Have a clear objective of what you want from each meeting or conversation. Start with the end result in mind.
>
> → Ask them how you can help them with their business and what they would like you to do.
>
> → E-mail them with an incentive shortly following the meeting to promote your business.
>
> → Ask them if they know anyone who would benefit from your services and if they would consider calling them in exchange for a financial incentive.
>
> → If you can, offer some free samples to show your confidence in your product or service.
>
> → Attend all business groups before deciding which one offers the best opportunities for business.

In summary, avoid underestimating the power of verbal communication. Some of the most successful entrepreneurs have grown their business empires based on third party referrals and the use of networking. The basic philosophy of networking is to treat everyone the way you would like to be treated.

Who Are Your Clients? No Really, Who Are Your Clients?

A successful entrepreneur knows their clients better than their clients they know themselves. However, from my experience some business owners fail to see the value of such information and so skip over this crucial step. Some even have the mind set that because they are only running a small business they don't have to be specific in their research methods. In fact, many unsuccessful business owners wrongly start a business venture without giving much thought to client research at all.

> **ASK YOURSELF**
>
> → How do you know your product offers the solution to your potential market?
>
> → Will your clients change with economic trends? If so, how?
>
> → Where your clients are geographically located and can you reach them?
>
> → How can you do this more efficiently?

If you haven't conducted any research to discover who your potential clients are, then how can you guarantee that they actually exist? Some business owners get carried away with dreams and concepts rather than reality and fact. As an entrepreneur you cannot afford to take the chance of selling to a non-existent market! Market research is normally divided into two separate types of research and is normally known as secondary and primary research.

The primary research serves to provide information through monitoring sales levels and measuring effectiveness of existing business practices such as service quality and tools for communication being used by the company. It carefully follows competitor plans to gather information on market competition. It rather acts like a feedback mechanism that assists you in the development in your business.

The secondary research consists of collecting already published data to create a "company database" that may serve to perform situation analysis. It helps to identify the company's competitors to perform a strategy for benchmarking. It also determines the segments the company should target in view of factors such as: demographics, population, usage rate, lifestyle and behavioural patterns. The secondary research in essence is the bit that establishes whether you have a market and if your business can actually run at a profit.

Imagine for a moment that you are about to open a high-end sushi restaurant called "Simply Sushi". You decide that your home town is an ideal place to open "Simply Sushi" since there isn't already a sushi restaurant in the area. You believe that this "Simply Sushi" is going to be a complete success based on the fact that it has no competitors in the area and because you yourself love the product. Your enthusiasm is increased after talking to friends and family as they think it's a fantastic idea and you are the right person for the job.

As your belief in "Simply Sushi" is so strong you move on to work on your business plan. After a meeting with the bank, they agree to give you a business loan secured on your personal assets. You secure premises in your local high street, although the rent is higher than you expected. You make these allowances as you assume that the risk is relatively low given that "Simply Sushi" is going to be an immediate hit!

After a brash attempt at market research you discover that the only places to eat in town are fast food and family owned restaurants, far from the high-end sushi restaurant you propose to open. Despite this you place adverts in local newspapers, put up billboards and deliver thousands of leaflets. You start to notice that you are investing large amounts of money up front as your bank balance diminishes. But again, you make allowances as you believe in your business making large profit margins once the restaurant is open.

After many sleepless nights, opening night finally arrives and you wait with baited breath for the large flock of diners you're expecting. You have prepared fully with balloons everywhere outside, flyers canvassing every car park in the area and you have run some of the biggest newspaper ads available.

It doesn't take long before you begin realize that something must have gone wrong. Only a couple of people trickle in and even then, when seeing the prices on the menu and the type of food you're offering, immediately head for the door. The people who do spend money that night are your family and friends who despite everything have come out to support you. You feel like a failure and cannot understand why your business is a flop. What you thought was low risk has actually turned out to be a high risk, causing you to waste time and more importantly lots of money.

> **Forewarned, forearmed, to be prepared is half the victory.**
>
> - Miguel de Cervantes

As far-fetched as this story might sound, this is a very common occurrence for business owners who start a business without conducting any research. Without knowing who your potential clients are, you can't possibly focus your business and marketing efforts in order to target them. It is like trying to shoot a gun with a blindfold on! If in the case of "Simply Sushi" both primary and secondary research was completed, it would have been established at the planning stage that the business was not a viable option.

While you may love sushi and have a passion to open that kind of business, you also need to consider seriously whether the area/marketplace is suitable for what you have to offer. You will find it difficult to persuade your clients to become something that they aren't. If they are families with little disposable income, then statistically they are not going to spend large amounts of money on sushi, but more of a buffet style restaurant.

In summary, market research is imperative for a company to know what type of products or services would be profitable to introduce in the market. Also with respect to its existing products in the market, good market research enables a company to know if it has been able to satisfy customer needs. Also whether any changes need to be made in the packaging, delivery or the product itself. This enables a company to formulate a viable marketing plan or measure the success of its existing plan.

Where Do They Go And What Do They Eat?

It may feel like overkill to assess where your potential clients go and what they eat, you may even believe that this is stalker behaviour! It does however, merely highlight the level of research that you need to do prior to starting your business venture. While observing their eating habits may not make a big difference in your kind of business, the point I am making is that you must understand more about your client than simply who they are.

If you have established during your preliminary research that you are targeting particularly young single women, then the places that you choose to display your advertising need to be the places where this audience is likely to see it. In other words, you wouldn't advertise in a fishing magazine (targeted at males aged between 30- 60) if you were targeting young single women.

Make sure you always keep to the specifics and avoid practicing general marketing. Avoid a scattergun approach and attempt to target everyone, just because this offers the biggest coverage of the market. Instead take a more strategic approach and target the exact client you want. Businesses that try and target everyone rarely deliver the message to the intended target audience. It is a very "hit and miss" method of marketing and generally turns out to be non cost-effective and a waste of money.

ASK YOURSELF

→ Where do your clients go to socialize, eat or work?

→ What type of employment are they in? (Manual labour, professional, work from home).

→ What kind of marketing incentives do they respond to? (Free trials, guarantees, coupons).

→ What publications do they read? (Local or national papers, trade papers, magazines).

Understanding your target market is one of the most important cornerstones of developing a strong marketing plan and a successful business. You have to explore and understand the emotions and attitude of your client base. Your marketing and advertising pieces should be directly related to those emotional triggers that will connect with your clients and motivate them to implement a call to action.

If you are struggling with the idea of marketing and this is not your forte, then it is an option to hire an external marketing business to do the job. Obviously this is at a cost. However, if you take the time to simply sit down and concentrate you'll be amazed how you can come up with some great ideas as to whom your target market is. Once you have established who your target market is, then go deeper by thinking about the types of things your target market wants and what you can offer them. Remember you must always market the solution to the problem and not the product or service.

ASK YOURSELF

What motivates your clients to buy your product or service?

How can this be relayed within your marketing?

There are two areas that you should focus your fact finding mission on. This will provide you with a more than acceptable detailed report on your clients.

Research Demographics:

Look at the age and gender of the people who use your product, this can be easily done by surveying the clients or deciding what age and gender you want to attract to your product. Find out your clients' education and income levels. You may be able to market differently to those who have earned a college degree versus those who haven't; and to those who are in a high income bracket versus those who aren't. Find out the marital status and family life cycle of your target clients, find out whether they are single, newlyweds, have been married for many years, or have children or grandchildren. Each relationship bracket of clients spends money differently.

Once you have completed the demographics of your clients, create a demographic profile. For example, you may find that your target market includes people in their 20s and 30s who graduated from high school, have a middle class income and are married with young children.

Research Psychographics:

The second part is to look at the target consumers' lifestyle. See whether they are conservative, trendy, or enjoy travelling. Every little detail can tell you the type of people they are and assist you to create the perfect marketing strategy. Figure out what social class your clients belong to: whether lower, middle or upper class. This tells you how much extra money they may have to spend and whether or not they spend it. Look at their activities, interests, attitudes and beliefs. Find out what they like to do in their spare time, what their hobbies are, what sort of music they listen to and whether they are interested in environmental issues or politics.

Put the psychographic information into a client's profile along with the demographic information to figure out who your market is and how to go about advertising to this market. Once you find this out, you can advertise to the people where they hang out, where they work out, go to eat or where they shop.

In a nutshell; if your target market is single women then you need to develop marketing pieces that have features and benefits that touch on those emotional hot points for that specific group of clients. Let's say that your business is a massage clinic. You would focus directly on the emotional triggers of a single woman such as being tired after a long day at work or trying to raise kids on their own. If you understand your target market then you will understand what affects them in such a way as to push them to purchase your product or service and be able to create an effective marketing message.

Whenever we are releasing a product I call upon friends who I trust to give critical feedback. If you know someone who fits the profile of your target client, you could ask them directly what they think as this avoids spending unnecessary money out of your marketing budget to advertise something that would fail to resonate with your client. Remember this is not your opinion; but is the opinion of the client that counts. Make sure that you establish who they, "actually are" rather than who you think they are.

The Chameleon In You – You Like Mickey Mouse? So Do I!

What makes chameleons so unique is obviously their ability to blend into any background. If they need to resemble tree bark, they can. If they need to resemble a brightly colored green leaf, they can do that too! As a successful entrepreneur, you will need to be as flexible as a chameleon. This means that you need to be able to quickly adapt to various situations and work comfortably with numerous types of clients with different personalities.

Entrepreneurs without a doubt are excellent communicators and know the importance of building trusting long term relationships with clients and fellow business owners. If you think about it you'll more than likely do something for someone you like and trust, than you would for someone you didn't. Having the ability to build rapport quickly is an essential tool as an entrepreneur, and you must become a master at it.

> **TOP TIP**
>
> Never go for Win-Lose always go for Win-Win. You and your client must always win within the deal.

Although there are many variations of the meaning of "rapport" in my World, it is simply the process of building a sustaining relationship of mutual trust, harmony and understanding. It is essentially meeting individuals in their model of the world; connecting with them on the same wavelength mentally and emotionally. Having rapport does not mean that you have to agree, but that you understand where the other person or people are coming from.

It's proven within any sales environment that entrepreneurs who have a more consultative selling approach are proven to do better in their marketplace.

This is largely due to the fact that they put people at ease and make them feel valued and not just a client. To start building rapport with clients you will need to be genuine. People are not stupid or naive and can tell when you're being fake or have your own intentions at heart. It is vital that you actually "care" about the needs and wants of your potential clients, not just your own benefits.

My top tip is that your business should never just be about your own financial gain, but should be about providing value and quality solutions to your clients. It's a basic rule that you are more likely to experience repeat business and referrals if your clients know you value their custom and not just their money. By being genuine, you build loyalty amongst your clients and ensure that your business is known as being morally strong.

A good way to do this is to imagine that your client's needs is that of either a friend or a family member, meaning that you should treat them in the same way. The old saying, "do unto others as you would have them do unto you" is especially true within a business atmosphere and generally creates a sense of self-fulfilment.

> " Perseverance is more prevailing than violence and many things which cannot be overcome when they are together yield themselves up when taken little by little. "
>
> - Plutarch

One of the biggest and most unnecessary faults of business owners and a big "No, No" within business is when they fail to respect the client's time. This is known in my World, as the ultimate rapport breaker and must never happen within your business. For instance, you must always be a little bit early or right on time for meetings and phone calls. Nothing is more unprofessional than being late. Being late shows a huge amount of disrespect and worse, inconveniences all parties involved. If you say that you're going to do something by a certain time then make sure you deliver this promise. Or better yet, you could meet deadlines early. In order to achieve this there is a saying "always under promise and over deliver".

Look at this way, suppose you are a mechanic for a moment. You tell the client that their car will be ready at 3 o'clock on Tuesday knowing that you can get the car ready by Monday morning. On the Monday morning you ring your client giving them the good news that their car is ready. You exceeded your client's expectations and so they are delighted with such a quick service. In this case the client is even relieved to be able to use their car again after the inconvenience of it breaking down in the first place. Not only this, you have allowed for any delays that may happen via external providers.

> **FACT**
>
> Marlboro was the first cigarette company to market a cigarette that had a red filter called "beauty tip". This was done to hide the lipstick marks left on the filter from women smokers wearing red lipstick.

In addition to building rapport with a client it would be advised to study their body language. Body language is a massive part of non-verbal communication that consists of body posture, gestures, facial expressions, and even eye movements. It can subconsciously reveal many clues as to the emotions felt by the client, but only if you know what to look for.

Here are a few obvious clues to look for:

✓ Tilting of head reflects interest or deep thought.

✓ Open palms reflect sincerity and openness.

✓ Biting nails reflects nervousness and the need to take action.

✓ Rubbing of hands reflects anticipation and the need for speed.

✓ Stroking of chin reflects trying to make a decision or internal reflection.

✓ Walking to and fro reflects urgency or impatience.

> ### TOP TIP
>
> If you are interested in learning more about body language, Google "Virginia Satir".

Another common method also used to build rapport with clients is by asking open-ended questions. Generally, some people find it difficult to be open with strangers in the beginning. To overcome this, it is important to remember that people love to talk about themselves, so this is a good starting point. People feel "touched" when you show an interest in them; this is especially true when you ask for a person's opinion. Ask open-ended questions that encourage conversation rather than those that can be answered yes or no when dealing with clients or when building rapport with others. It can often work as an effective tool to overcome any suspicion about your objective.

For example: instead of asking "Is your business is going well?" You should ask them "How is your business going?" They may answer "Fine," but it at least gives you the opportunity to further conversation by asking a question such as: "What kinds of marketing campaigns are working for your business at the moment?"

Another great way of breaking down barriers or initial shyness with a potential client is using what is known as the feel, felt, found technique. This technique is mainly used when your client objects or has a negative feeling about something. You emphasize with the client and understand where they are "coming from". Only once you earn their "trust" will you then have the ability to assist them effectively. This method can work in so many different ways even in the parenting of children!

For example: "I know exactly how you feel, I felt the same way myself at first.

I thought X-business was just a catalogue job for people who wanted to earn a little extra pocket money. I had no idea that it was a network marketing business, where its employees were earning good money. There's no way a couple of years ago I'd have even considered it, but after being shown the opportunity in detail, what I found was that the reality is very different from what I had initially thought."

In summary, there is a saying: "It is not how much you know, it is the people that you know that will help you to succeed." I agree that knowledge is essential, but knowing the right people and developing good rapport with them is the key to success.

4 - Building A Business, Not An Income

4 Building A Business, Not An Income

Sustainable Business Planning – Allocate Monthly Thinking Time

The majority of small business owners run on what I call "habitual patterning" when it comes to day-to-day working. In my World, this is one of the main reasons that business owners miss the potential opportunities open to them even when they are staring them right in the face.

> **ASK YOURSELF**
>
> Have you ever been driving home, and suddenly realized that you arrived without remembering the whole journey? This best describes the "state" and how easily time and information can be deleted from your mind.

It's important to understand that the original functions of habits are to simplify our lives. However, many of these unhelpful habits can be traced back to our childhood and are therefore not necessarily correct. It is essential as an entrepreneur to be very aware of negative habits and make sure that you avoid falling into the trap of "blind sailing". In my World, the state of "habitual patterning" should be regarded as being one of the least effective mental states within business.

Spending your life, and more importantly your business time, within this auto-pilot state will be the demise of your business. Therefore if your business is growing slowly or not making a profit, then it's likely that you can expect those same results to continue happening year after year based on this state alone.

From observing many business owners while in this state, one thing is apparent. They tend to be oblivious to opportunities that could massively improve the success of their business, simply because they are not actively looking for them. In some cases they often miss certain market changes that have devastating effects on their profits. The success of any business is reliant on the entrepreneur being constantly, mentally aware of their business, their surroundings and consciously being out of the negative state of "habitual patterning".

>
> **TOP TIP**
>
> Business planning should not be a once a year thought! Do it monthly and call it a monthly "business check-up" if you like. This type of planning will massively increase your chances of business development and personal fulfilment.

A great way to avoid running your business in this state of "habitual patterning" is by utilizing your business plan. Remember your business plan should not be a static document. In the process of maintaining your business plan you should be reminded to look for (and so be constantly aware of) those critical points within your business such as market changes and business opportunities.

Taking the time each month to sit down and re-evaluate is vitally important in the success of your business, and will decrease the chances of falling into this state for more than is necessary.

If you have identified a state of negative "habitual patterning" then here are some simple tips to break any habits affecting your business or your life:

Focus on one habit at a time:

It is said that habits are formed after doing something 10,000 times. Avoid focusing on changing any more than one habit at a time, as one is going to be enough. Make a plan to change your habit within no more than 30 days, after this time a new habit would have been sufficiently conditioned.

Have a fun trigger:

A trigger is a short ritual you perform before a habit, also known as a pattern interrupt. If for example you wanted to avoid using the word "try" every time you would normally use this word change it to the word "fart". A trigger helps condition a new pattern more consistently and changes the physiological association with the habit. Notice the difference when you say "I will try and increase the number of sales this month." to "I will fart and increase the number of sales this month." Have fun with this exercise and notice the difference within your neurology simply by changing the words that you use on a regular basis.

Fill the void:

Like most things in life, when you give something up there is a void that is going to have to be filled. Have a conversation out loud with yourself about the reasons why you did what you did and ask yourself: "What can I do to fulfil this need in a positive way?"

Get your language right:

A great way to any form of positive change is to improve the language that you use or associate with that issue or task. Rather than using language patterns like: "I can't change that state." use positive language patterns like: "How can I change this state and really enjoy the process?" This simple change process re-aligns your mind to think about the positive in all solutions, and can radically change the way you look at all tasks in your personal and professional life.

Get in down on paper:

Avoid leaving commitments in your brain. Always get your habitual changes down on paper. This does two things. First, it creates clarity by defining in specific terms what your change means. Second, it keeps you committed since it is easy to dismiss a thought, but harder to dismiss a promise printed in front of you.

Get leverage:

People often complete tasks if there is some form of betterment associated with achieving a task. Offer yourself a reward if you make the change, anything to give yourself that extra push. If there is more than one task then reward yourself for each task achieved, and a larger one for completing the whole series of tasks.

Keep it simple:

Your change should involve one or two rules, not a dozen. Simple rules create habits, complex rules create headaches. Keep your strategy simple and easy to follow. Imagine writing the plan with steps aimed at a seven year old. This will avoid further procrastination.

Create consistency:

The point of an installed habit is that it doesn't require thought, where things happen naturally. To change a habit you must make sure your new habit is as consistent as possible. Repeat it every day until it doesn't need a pre-thought to action. This will ensure a new habit is drilled in.

Tell everyone:

Once you have identified the habit that you want to change, and have written it down; share it with friends, colleagues or family members. Ask them to make you accountable for your actions. Start a is social media website, post your habitual change there and ask friends for regular check ups.

Another way in which you could ensure that you avoid running in a "negative state" is to consistently brainstorm ways in which you could potentially improve your business. These ideas often don't come during the time you allocate to brainstorming. It is advisable to always have a notepad and pen handy for the times when you do suddenly have these ideas. I keep one in my pocket at all times and later transfer all ideas onto our office "ideas wall". Here the rest of the team add their views and personal inspiration. This spurs off the original idea and may create a better way of putting the product to the market.

> **Time is our most valuable asset, yet we tend to waste it, kill it, and spend it rather than invest it.**

- Jim Rohn

In summary, make the commitment to change your negative habits that are not complementing you or your business as these are likely to keep you from the success you deserve.

Selling to the Next Generation – Talk To Teachers And Parents

In many cases, business owners can be oblivious when it comes to client bases outside of their target audience. They become complacent in only knowing who their current clients are and so apply all of their marketing efforts and attention on these. These business owners fail to realize the potential to increase their client base and opportunities by simply adapting their product/services in order to create a much longer-term, sustainable income source. It is vital to remember that business is not simply about right "now" but the effectiveness of your business in the future. Although the "present" is obviously important to pay your bills and have an income, creating a successful business involves setting up your business for your legacy.

A common example of this is where a business fails to target a young audience. Young audiences are the future clients in every possible sense and should be at the forefront of every entrepreneur. Once "hooked" they will most likely be buying into your brand right through into adulthood. Therefore, they will not require a convincing marketing strategy at a later date. Clients often stick to what they know, so my tip is to catch them early! In order to attract this audience, business owners must be aware of new technology and innovations. Typically, young audiences thrive on the latest trends, gismos and gadgets. Keeping tabs on what is going to be popular in the future will help you to prepare your business for this market.

Like everything in business, to be able to target this audience you will first need to research them. Study their activities, buying habits and more importantly; find out what it is exactly they want. "Apple" in my World, is the best example of a business that conducts its market research primarily on the future generations. Apple owes most of its success to knowing exactly what their young clients want (new and exciting products) and are taking massive action to achieve it. They recognize that in order to offer their clients these new and exciting products they have to be constantly at the forefront of innovation. Therefore they focus all of their resources on attracting this type of client.

Apple has a fantastic branding strategy that focuses on the emotions of their clients. The Apple brand personality is about: lifestyle, imagination, liberty regained, innovation, passion, hopes, dreams, aspirations and power-to-the-people through technology. The Apple brand personality is also about: simplicity and the removal of complexity from people's lives with people-driven product design. Apple is about being a really humanistic company with a heartfelt connection with its clients.

In summary, studying and marketing to the younger generation will always lead to new ideas, progressive thinking and a better chance of sustaining a future income. Spend some time visualizing your future and incorporating it within your legacy.

Affiliate Schemes – Sell Yourself, Products and Services

Ask yourself what would happen if you were to get sick, take a vacation or have a family emergency that meant you had to take time away from your business? Is it likely that your business would stall or even terminate completely? Have you thought about the means in which you could generate profits without you even having to be present? Have you got a solid back-up plan?

Most entrepreneurs begin a business venture with a reason in mind based around one of the three key motivators mentioned in Chapter One, but over time these motivators can be forgotten and commonly change to a strong desire of freedom. This freedom can be measured in many different ways depending on your lifestyle but include: the escape from the strict 9 to 5 working hours, freedom from the hour-long commute each morning and evening, but most commonly, the freedom of not feeling guilty about having to leave early. Unfortunately, once a business is running most business owners actually become handcuffed to it, taking little or (in some cases) no time out.

In these cases, the business has been set up so that it is unable to make profits without the owners constant presence. Consequently, these business owner's actually end up working more hours, missing more family functions and earning less income in the process. Basically everything and more of what they aimed to avoid!

One method that you should consider to avoid this happening within your business is what is known as an affiliate scheme. An affiliate scheme is a marketing practice in which a business rewards one or more affiliates for each client that is brought about by the affiliate's own efforts. In other words, the affiliates work to sell the business and in return the business rewards them with a small cut of the profit they generate. These affiliates are often businesses that are related to the industry. So they are interested in selling similar products/services that they do not offer but see a demand. The reward is often financial and works on commission basis. For example every item an affiliate sells they receive as little as 5% to 10% of the value of the item they are selling, increasing to up to 50% in some cases.

There are two ways in which an affiliate scheme should be considered for your business:

Sign up to an external affiliate scheme:

External affiliate marketing is where you sell other businesses' products and earn money based on how much you sell. When signing up to an external affiliate scheme there are a few things to consider:

It is logical and is often a better source of income to choose a business that offers products similar to those that your business offers. You are already marketing and attracting that type of audience. Therefore you are just offering an addition to the products associated with your own.

> **FACT**
>
> Americans write approximately 50 billion cheques a year making it the second most frequent payment method used after cash.

Your choice should also fall in line with your business morals and ethics. Meaning you, yourself believe in the product and are comfortable in representing that product on your site. You need to make sure that you choose a product that complements your products and doesn't make your business appear hypocritical or disrespectful. For example, if you are a business offering health foods you wouldn't choose an affiliate scheme whereby you promoted cigarette packets.

Here are some things to consider why signing up to an affiliate scheme may be beneficial to your business:

The first and probably the most obvious is that as an affiliate seller you do not need to create your own product. The business (merchant) takes care of that for you. For this reason you are able to get started very quickly as an affiliate marketer, making money online once you have joined the merchant's affiliate program.

Most affiliate marketing programs are free to join. It is obviously good for the affiliate marketer (you) because there is no financial risk involved in signing up to the program. If it doesn't work you can just change to another until you find one that works well with your business.

Affiliate merchants make it very easy for their affiliates to make money online. They provide everything: the marketing materials, they collect the money, deal with product shipping and customer service.

In my World, the biggest benefits of affiliate marketing is the opportunity it gives you to earn money 24 hours a day. Unlike a traditional business you do not have to open a physical store to sell products. On the Internet sales are not dictated by your personal working hours but by how savvy you are. Remember although this may not be a long term objective, you can utilize the money earnt within affiliate marketing to grow and develop your own products.

Creating your own affiliate scheme:

This is where you create a scheme and invite other business owners to promote your products in exchange for commission. There are hundreds if not thousands of online packages available that allow you to create your own affiliate scheme. Affiliates simply sign up online, start selling your products and the program works out the shares and transfers the correct amount of money to the right accounts on a monthly basis. All you have to do is authorize the payment.

> " Your own mind is a sacred enclosure into which nothing harmful can enter except by your permission. "
>
> - Ralph Waldo Emerson

The best way to understand how an affiliate scheme does this is to think about the workings of an ant-hill. Every day, hundreds, if not thousands, of ants work on building the ant-hill. In looking at the infrastructure of the ant-hill you understand that: The ant-hill has been built gradually with one grain at a time. The ant-hill could not have been built as quickly by one ant alone. When you really think about it, the amount of work that goes into creating such a large structure for such a small creature is almost unimaginable.

Logically the more affiliates that you have within your affiliate scheme (the ants), the more items overall they are going to sell. Therefore the more profit you are going to receive (the bigger the hill). When you combine the profits these affiliates generate altogether for your business, the income that you could receive could be potentially quite substantial compared to what you could have done alone; especially when starting out.

I believe that no matter what is happening within the economy you will always have to think globally rather than just locally, laterally opposed to horizontally. Expand the options to earn additional income; especially when it comes to online sales or marketing. By creating an affiliate network, you reduce the amount of work you have to do on your own, while increasing your income substantially through the work of other people.

Before creating your own affiliate scheme you may want to consider a few things. With any technical service, you will still need a member of support or customer service staff on hand to answer any queries regarding the affiliate scheme. Affiliates may have questions about your products or services, or they may have an issue with receiving their payment. Make sure that you have thought through the complete costing and return of this income. Work out if it is an effective means for the initial start up costs. You certainly don't want to create more work for yourself since an affiliate program is supposed to free your time. This responsibility once up and running could be delegated to one of your current employees, but you can also hire specialists (normally overseas call centres) who are experienced at managing affiliates. If you decide to use an employee then it is advisable to ensure that they are suitably trained to perform this job without supervision, and have the answers to any potential questions that may arise.

> **FACT**
>
> The Nike swoosh was invented by Caroline Davidson back in 1971. She received £35 for making the swoosh. The first shoe with the swoosh was introduced in 1972.

You will also need to provide some basic marketing tools for your affiliates to use to market your products/services. Items such as banner advertisements and product pictures along with information about your products or services. Getting the proper information and training to your affiliates is the key to having a successful program. Invest time into your affiliate program and make sure to include PDF downloads or videos to explain your products or services and simple steps showing how they can sign up. The better equipped your affiliates are the more likely they are going to be able to and want to promote your business. Not only will the affiliate scheme create an income during the time you take off. If will also allow you to reach profit goals that you may have initially thought impossible.

Here are a few reasons why your business should consider offering an affiliate scheme as part of its growth and development:

Cost-effective customer acquisition:

There is no payment to affiliates unless they refer a visitor who subsequently becomes a client. This is a great way to build a database of pre-qualified clients who have the potential to also become affiliates and promote your business.

Fixed costs:

The commission paid to affiliates is normally a percentage of the sale. You set the commission, and you pay when sales are made. There aren't any variables beyond that; unless you choose to pay different levels of commission as sales increase.

Brand visibility:

Affiliates can secure high search engine listings and/or display your ads on their website. This is all free brand exposure and a great benefit of affiliate marketing. If several of your clients have good page rankings this can capture the market share for specific keywords.

Outsourced marketing teams:

Many affiliates are experts in search engine marketing, providing you with a way of potentially getting to the top of Google without needing to spend a fortune on SEO (Search Engine Optimisation).

Find-ability:

With the above point in mind, if a consumer visits Google and multiple listings ultimately link to you, then you're going to have a much better chance of being found than competitors with only one or two (or no) links on the first page.

Transparency:

A key appeal for businesses is the transparency of return on investment, through the ability to track the origin of sales. You can see exactly where and when sales are made and consider whether this form of marketing warrants further investment.

In summary, affiliate marketing can be a viewed as a win-win situation for both the marketer and the affiliate. Working together, they can be an advantage to both financially. Affiliate marketing is one of the most basic and most efficient business opportunities on the Internet today. Make sure that you seriously consider how it may assist your business.

Don't Borrow, Save – Invest In Your Business Monthly

One of the most common mistakes that business owners make especially in the initial stages of a business is spending far too much money on "stuff" rather than re-investing their future. All too often these eager business owners saturate their own funds and those borrowed from an external company (usually a bank) until re-investment seems like an unachievable task.

In today's financial climate it can be very easy to fall into debt, borrowing after borrowing until your business is forced into bankruptcy. It is far more beneficial and expected as an entrepreneur to reserve and later reinvest some of the profits back into the business. This maintains future profits and so avoids bankruptcy altogether. Although this appears obvious, many business owners neglect this and often suffer unnecessarily.

Business owners who allow their business to build up a large debt restrict their options if a business experiences problems with finances or finds fantastic business opportunities in the future. The successful "debt free" entrepreneurs are often the ones that work on a "shoestring" budget. They spend money only when necessary and reinvest the reserved profits when it is financially viable. Part of your business plan should include how and on what you plan to reinvest a cut of your profits every month. Thus allowing you to grow your revenue more rapidly and secure a sustainable future for your business. Within this area of your business plan you should also include exactly the percentage of each month's profits you plan to reinvest and how it can be measured. This will give you a rough indication of the amount of money you expect to "play with" when you choose what and how to reinvest in. Remember sustainability is essential within the world of business.

> **FACT**
>
> The first product to ever be scanned with a bar code was Wrigley's gum on June 26, 1974.

From experience the most successful entrepreneurs tend to work on a "pay as they go" basis and continually reinvest in themselves and their business. In the process they carefully monitor the most effective sources of income and those that are not. I believe that careful monitoring of any business re-investment may not play an important part when the economy is strong; but if implemented is more effectively proven to be essential when the economy takes a downturn. Businesses that know their outgoings and what their returns are on those outgoings are the ones that will always survive. It's simple mathematics, the less you borrow, the less you owe and lower your repayments. Thereby the more flexibility you have to re-invest in more revenue incomes.

With each re-investment that you make it is essential that you measure the success or feedback based on the results you receive. Avoid falling into the trap of believing the more you spend the more you get back, as this is rarely the case. Looking at the effectiveness of an investment (time, money, attitude and so on) is known as "return on investment" (ROI). This is something that the larger companies go to great lengths to evaluate and reflect. For some reason small business owners who are worried about cash flow, fail to identify

ROI as a valuable need. Working out the ROI is a must for smaller business and is especially important when dealing with small or tight profit margins.

There are many areas where ROI is used to measure the predicted effectiveness of each pound/time spent. Advertising is the most common; some business owners view advertising as a business expense when it should really be considered an investment in your business. If done correctly, the money spent on spreading the word about your business should come back to you tenfold. Though it doesn't make sense to spend thousands on an ad that will only generate a few hundred pounds in sales, it does make sense to focus your efforts and spend what you know you can earn back.

ASK YOURSELF

 Would your business benefit from updated machinery so that you can produce products faster and at an improved quality?

 What can you do to invest in a new business venture that complements your original business?

For example: if you spent £100 on a classified ad in a publication that reaches your target customer base and your average customer spends £20, you need only five people to respond to the ad to make it worth the investment. And don't forget about repeat business and the value of up-sales. If you have a quality product or service, your clients should return again and again so you can afford to invest even more to attract new clients.

In summary, it is important to understand that it is unlikely that your company will become a "money-spinner overnight". It is therefore more beneficial to wisely invest your time and money into growing the business from the roots, steadily and gradually. Remembering that the foundations are the most fundamental part. You can think of this in terms of a physical building, if the foundations on which a house is built are unstable then eventually that house will fall down! This process requires a lot of perseverance and patience, but the later benefits will make it worthwhile. Remember, Rome wasn't built in a day! Use your profits to their full advantage to generate further profits rather than just debt servicing. Make sure that you measure the effectiveness of each of your actions.

Create More Income Streams – Sell Your Competitor's Products

It may seem against the principle of business to think about selling and promoting your competitor's products or services and I have been ridiculed in the past. However, entrepreneurs must think laterally rather than being narrow minded in order for their business to survive, particularly during the initial stages of business or economic downturns. I have earned tens of thousands of pounds by selling competitor's products, which I simply reinvested in growing my business. Ultimately leap-frogging those very competitors.

> **FACT**
>
> There is now an ATM at McMurdo Station in Antarctica, which has a winter population of two hundred people.

It is important to understand that you cannot be all things to all clients. In other words it would be virtually impossible for you to have the means or sometimes the money to offer every product and service that a client requires at times. You may just have to accept that your competitor's products or services may be better suited to the target audience or are more financially worthwhile than your own. Avoid having an adversarial mindset when it comes to your competitors as this can be their weakness and should not be yours. Start thinking about how you can make use of their products to satisfy your clients and still earn a cut of the profits.

For example: Let's say you specialize in building custom racing bicycles. You own a bicycle shop called "Bikes Galore" in which you sell your bikes. Some of your clients are racing fanatics and so are interested in paying the high price for your custom built bikes. On the other hand some clients are looking for a basic bicycle to go on the odd bike ride at the weekend with the family.

These clients are less likely to buy your own expensive bikes. But why lose their custom? "Raleigh," produce bikes in bulk thanks to their investment in manufacturing machinery and you can buy them at a cheap wholesale price. Why not inflate this price and take the difference as profit every time that type of customer comes into your shop and buys that product?

Don't lose out on sales because of feelings of pride or significance. You need to make sure that you cater for the wider audience at all times. Another way to achieve this is by branching out into offering products that complement your initial business. Going back to "Bikes Galore" you could offer bicycle accessories including helmets, lights, and pumps and so on. The list is endless.

If you do decide to sell a competitor's products, then make sure you choose the companies that have already invested large amounts of money on refining their products, branding and marketing. As with "Bikes Galore", "Raleigh" is a well-known established brand that in effect sells itself. Clients are far more likely to buy a familiar brand than one that they don't recognize. Take advantage of this free marketing! You may even be able to "transfer" some of this brand loyalty and validity onto your own business in time. If a client trusts their brand and you are representing them, then your clients will naturally assume that your own products are of the same calibre, if not better.

FACT

 One survey revealed product categories with personal loyalties of over fifty percent: cigarettes, mayonnaise, toothpaste, coffee, headache remedy, film, bath soap and ketchup. Reasons varied from flavour and taste - ketchup and cigarettes; to image - beer, cigarettes and perfume.

It's a well known fact that retaining an existing client is often more profitable than finding a new client. Although at some stage you may move away from your competitor's products, it is important to consider the initial financial impact on your business; and the future opportunities to up-sell your own products when those clients return.

Virgin is a brand in the US, which is offers financial services, cola drinks, music and an airline, and the brand is doing well in all of these categories. This is because the clients feel that the time invested in learning about the brand has resulted in a positive outcome. Thus, an experience in one is assumed to be the same in another.

In summary, the advantages of customer loyalty are more pronounced in a downturn. Loyal clients cost less to serve and they typically concentrate more spending with companies they trust. Utilize larger more well know companies within your industry to transfer their client brand loyalty over to you with a clear strategy within your business plan.

How Are They Going To Remember You – Trusted Consultant!

No matter what industry you are in, your success is determined on how your clients perceive you as an individual, your brand or in fact every client "touch point". At some point you may need to personally sell your products or services. In this sense you, yourself may be judged. Personally there is a fine line separating someone who is considered a trusted consultant (one that has your best interests in mind) and one who is perceived as a salesperson (one that is interested in making profits). However, one is viewed in a lot higher regard than the other.

ASK YOURSELF

 Think about how you feel when a telemarketer calls you and starts reading from a script.

 Do you think that this person cares about what you actually want? Or do you think that this person just wants to make a profit out of your custom?

The general public just like you, hate to be sold to and often turn down sales calls or pitches before they hear what is being sold. The world in general has begun to stereotype the majority of salespeople as those only interested in making money and often are untrustworthy. This is why it is very important that you present the correct image showing that you are in fact, a trusted consultant and not just another salesperson.

FACT

Every year, Dunkin' Donuts serves an estimated 650 million cups of coffee.

So, how do you become a trusted consultant instead of a salesperson? As you may already know a consultant is someone that provides expert advice on a particular industry, such as a doctor, lawyer or banker. Like them, once experience is gained and a good knowledge is achieved; then you should consider yourself to be an "Industry Expert/Trusted Consultant". It goes without saying that you must always be truthful and direct your client to the most suitable choice for them, and not the one that generates the most profit for you. This simple linguistic shift from "Salesperson/Business Owner" to "Trusted Consultant/Industry Expert" creates a whole different meaning to your clients, and changes their perception on your abilities to achieve and provide.

Once you have made the shift in your industry "title" you should also consider what physical actions you should change. To ensure you do this effectively, I recommend that you actively listen to the needs of your client. (Although many business owners think they listen, they actually are just listening to what they want to hear). Ask them lots of questions so that you clearly define what it is they want to achieve. Avoid half listening and then assuming what the client is going to say. Clients like to feel that you have listened and understood fully their problems and requirements. Once you know these, narrow down the options you have available and offer the most appropriate. Many successful entrepreneurs involved within the sales industry will tell you that selling products should be about problem solving, finding the best answer to a problem, and not simply about selling as much as you can.

> **TOP TIPS**
>
> → Take action on what you say you are going to do. Possibly the most important step to building a foundation of trust is to do what you say you will do. Even if it is a small thing, cancelling or failing to follow through will create hairline fractures in your trustworthiness.
>
> → Obviously never lie. Sounds easy! Not always. It's surprisingly simple to find yourself saying a little white lie to protect your business. But if you tell the truth even when the truth isn't perfectly pleasant, you will become much more trustworthy. Remember people will always find out the truth in the end. This can cause a string of failures with future business.
>
> → Don't mask truths. An off-shoot of "Never lie" is never to mask truths. Sometimes it seems harmless to "morph" the truth into something more palatable to preserve your ego. If you don't know something then "say so". Your clients will respect you for not knowing something rather than masking it.
>
> → Show openness. This implies relying on a person to give you the full truth and avoids them holding back information which may be important in your business decision.

Further to this, never forget that your clients have the power of what is known as "the word of mouth". They have control over what they tell their friends or family and in fact anyone that they meet. For example: one customer said while talking to her friend: "I bought a TV set in that electrical store last week. I think it's called "Electrical Central," anyway the sales person said that I needed all these extra cables to make it work in my house. But when I got home my husband said that I didn't need them at all. I don't think I will go back to that store again and I don't think you should unless you want to be ripped off!"

This client has now shared their negative experiences with a friend who now could share these feelings with one of their friends and so on. This would most likely lead to a decrease in your custom all resulting from one dissatisfied client. On the flip side this could work for positive experiences and you could see a rise in custom as positive feelings have been spread about your business.

TOP TIPS

- Show consistency in your behaviour. This relates to your reliability and predictability. It also determines your ability and good judgement in handling situations. This will ensure what your clients experience on all occasions especially when recommending others to your business.

- Display loyalty. This refers to your ability to protect others, to be on same side, in their presence but most importantly in their absence. Avoid discussing past client's disapproval or issues with other business owners.

- Demonstrate a strong moral ethic. This is particularly important in building lasting relationships. The other person must feel confident that you will not falter or show betrayal in any form, when away from the other. People must not doubt your ability to be true or dedicated.

Due to many untrustworthy salespeople, clients have now learnt to be sceptical when it comes to parting with their money. One negative experience or comment about your business is enough for them to avoid your business altogether. In order to build a high income, long-lasting business, you need to become a client's lifetime trusted consultant within your industry and the first business they come to every time they want advice. Remember they are more likely to return if you are honest and they know they can trust you.

Most property estate agents set a good example when it comes to being a trusted consultant. Their business often depends solely upon focusing their efforts on creating a lifelong business partnership with their clients. It's true that some property estate agents simply work to receive commission from a client and move on. However, if you think about how much it costs to generate one lead that turns into a client; then it makes sense that if you can become their trusted consultant and have a lifetime source of income from that particular client. Then you have saved money in the long run on generating new leads.

In summary taking the salesperson, hard sell approach is no longer effective. Instead you should be taking the role of a trusted consultant, listening to the client, asking about their problems and then providing them with the best solution. This is of course, regardless of your own short-term financial gain as it will instead provide you with a more profitable long-term financial gain.

Time Isn't Free And It Doesn't Help The Cash Flow

As an entrepreneur you need to understand that your time is not free. Why do you think it is called "spending" time? In fact time is one of the things you have in common with your competitors. Spending time wisely is key in the successful running of a business. Your time is actually extremely valuable. "Spending" precious time creating flyers, organizing meetings and filing paperwork are generally not considered to be high-income earning tasks. They are certainly not what you, as an entrepreneur, should be focusing your efforts on.

> **FACT**
>
> Retail sales for soft drinks in the United States in 2001 were more than sixty billion dollars.

Part of running a successful business is learning how to manage your time effectively. As entrepreneur and head visionary, you, yourself should be focused on the tasks that generate the most income and create the best forward momentum in the business. Any other tasks are considered to be administrative and therefore are best outsourced or delegated.

Being organized is one method you can use to ensure that you utilize your time effectively. For example: you could be organized so that you know what task needs doing next and therefore you don't waste time in between tasks. You could even have your paperwork organized, so that when you are looking for a certain file you know exactly where to find it and you haven't lost time looking for it. If you struggle with organization skills then you might want to ask or hire someone to help.

Spend at least 15 minutes everyday prioritizing your tasks in a "to-do" list. Spending this initial small amount of time to set daily goals will save you more time throughout the day and so make you more efficient. All high priority tasks on your "to-do" list need to be an actual appointment written in your calendar or diary. Your calendar or diary is a tool used to remind yourself of where you need to be and at what time. So when an appointment is written down you will be more committed to keeping it, as it's a lot harder to ignore or avoid doing.

If you still have trouble remembering to check and update your written calendar or diary; then you may want to consider using a time management software program on your computer. There are many variations of these programs that offer different features, so you may need to test a few of them until you find the right one for you. For example: some of these programs have a feature that will set of an alarm and so alert you to a task that needs to be done. Some of these features you may find useful and some you may never use.

Often a digital calendar can be found on your phone. Obviously this depends on your type of phone. One of the main features that a phone calendar has is to send SMS text reminders to yourself to remind you of certain task.

In conclusion, in order for your business to be successful you need to use your time wisely and efficiently. There is no excuse for not being organized within your business especially as there are now many tools (thanks to new technology) for you to utilize. The more organized you are, the clearer your mindset.

CHAPTER 4 BUILDING A BUSINESS, NOT AN INCOME

> **ASK YOURSELF**
>
> → When assessing how time management figures into your daily business activities, it's important to ask yourself some questions to see how you are utilizing your time.
>
> → Do you find yourself often procrastinating? Are there certain tasks that you are uncomfortable doing such as cold calling or setting up speaking engagements to advertise your business?
>
> → Are you avoiding those things that will generate more business because of a fear or anxiety?
>
> → Do you have a clear-cut "to-do" list that you work from each day? Do you check off the items throughout the day that have been done to give yourself a feeling of accomplishment?
>
> → Do you create a calendar/schedule that keeps you on task to get the things done that will bring in more business and income?
>
> → Are you well versed in dealing with interruptions during your day? Do you allow things to get you completely off-track and forget what you were doing before the interruption?
>
> → Are you able to delegate effectively? Are you able to set the monotonous tasks to an employee so that you can focus on the more important parts of your business?

5 - Know Your Product Or Service

5 Know Your Product Or Service

Is Your Product Better, Worse or Different?

Two questions that all good business owners should ask themselves are: "How good is my product or service?" and "How is my product or service different from those offered by my competitors?" Knowing the answer to these questions greatly assists in establishing "how" your product or service can be delivered to the target market. In my World, without it you're simply providing the market with another choice rather than a valuable solution.

A method that can be used to help answer these questions and later can be utilized within your marketing image, is to establish your USP. The term USP (Unique Selling Point/Proposition) is basically the factor or consideration presented by a business as a clear reason why their brand, product or service is different from and better than that of the competition. This is communicated within marketing material to persuade clients to choose them over another.

Before getting started on creating a USP for your business, it is important to understand that no matter how much you think it is, your business is unlikely to be a one-of-a kind or unique. In order to create the illusion that your business is, and to stand out in a crowded market, you must communicate an effective, memorable and unique USP. Entrepreneurialism in this sense is more about making your brand, product or service appear strictly unique to the client rather than re-inventing the wheel.

In this day and age with lots of scepticism within the market, clients need to be shown a good reason and convincing proposition as to why they should be buying into your brand rather than someone else's. If you fail to present a good enough reason to your clients, then it is likely that they won't even consider your brand, products or services within their choices. Obviously the consequences of this can be catastrophic. To ensure you aren't forgotten about, I would highly recommend spending some time each month to consider what makes your brand, products or services more valuable and unique than your competitor's. Then incorporate this within your current marketing material.

CHAPTER 5 KNOW YOUR PRODUCT OR SERVICE

> "He who reigns within himself and rules his passions, desires, and fears is more than a king"
>
> - John Milton

A great example of effective and clear USP is the one used by FedEx. "Federal Express: When it absolutely, positively has to be there overnight." This USP clearly indicates the advantage the customer will receive if they choose to take their custom to FedEx. Although many other couriers are also physically able to offer overnight delivery, they don't concentrate on communicating this in their marketing. Therefore, they lose out on potential clients with that particular need.

There are often many advantages or reasons to buy a product or service. Yet from experience, many businesses fail to advertise this to potential clients. In my World, the best way is to create a USP that is the both unique compared to your competitors, but also is most attractive to your client. Avoid using the basic functions of your product or services as these are often expected. For example if selling a car you wouldn't advertize that the car gets you from A to B. You would instead advertize that it gets you there in comfort and in style, and play on the emotions attached to owning the product.

A USP is largely based on the image you give to your client rather than the physical product or service. Avoid getting carried away by communicating an over-the-top USP, as a ridiculous or far-fetched USP could deter clients as it may sound too good to be true. For example: "The Only Business Formula In The World To Earn You One Million Dollars." If your statement does include a statement that could be interpreted as something bordering on the elaborate or far-fetched then you should offer proof within your USP; as this will reduce scepticism. For example: "Proven Success Secrets from Multimillionaire Entrepreneur." Also be cautious about the claims that you make within your USP. If you underperform after such a big claim then it is likely that you will discourage repeat custom, and clients will only be disappointed. So, doing something less unachievable should be considered to avoid any embarrassment.

Here are a several tips that we use within our business ventures on how to establish a powerful USP, and how you could consider incorporating them within your marketing material:

Think about your product or service from a client's perspective:

Remember, as an entrepreneur your opinion of your products or service is irrelevant. The love most entrepreneurs have for their own products and services often clouds their view of what their clients actually think. Don't forget that the client's view is the most significant. Take a step back from your business and scrutinize it from a client's view. If you still struggle to do this then "shop" your competitors.

> **FACT**
>
> During the holiday season, approximately £220 million worth of Poinsettias are sold.

Many retailers do this to find out what and how their competitors are selling and how good or bad the customer service is. This is better known as "mystery shopping". By doing this you can understand personally the shopping experience discovering aspects you liked and which you didn't. Particularly, the factors you didn't like could be improved within your own business and therefore used as your USP.

Know what it is that motivates your client's buying decisions:

It is not enough to know basic demographics of your clients. You need to really know what makes your clients "tick". In other words you may be required to learn a little psychology. You may be surprised to know that clients are rarely motivated by price. There are in fact many factors that can affect a client's buying habits. These can include: taste, peer pressure, convenience and desired lifestyles.

The most common of these is demonstrated within the advertisements produced by the cosmetic and liquor industries. These industries are based on a desire factor of a product and not its functionality or price. These advertisements evoke feelings of luxury and glamour. They are selling the lifestyle rather than the product itself. So find out what your clients want your product to accomplish in their lives.

ASK YOURSELF

→ What motivates your clients to buy your product or service right now?

→ How will it make them feel by owning your product?

→ Does it make them feel sexier to their mate?

→ Does it accomplish other goals by saving them time or money?

Uncover the real reasons your clients buy your product or service and not your competitor's:

Your clients are the best source of information. Create questionnaires or run focus groups to find out why you clients come to you. Is there one particular reason that makes you stand out against your competitors, and if so could it be used as your USP?

Keep it short and sweet:

An effective USP is brief and concise. It should be one sentence only. This is not about creating a long paragraph or a 5-page report. Remember a USP is communicated within advertising, so you will only have a window of just a couple of seconds to capture the attention of your target audience. Take all of the information you discovered within the previous steps and create one sentence that sums up everything for the customer. If you've done it correctly; your USP should generate initial interest and so make the client want to actively find out more.

Only one USP at a time:

Your advertising campaigns must concentrate on one USP at a time. This is to avoid confusion with the client. It is easier for your clients to focus on and remember one good reason to buy your product or service rather than being bombarded with multiple messages. As mentioned earlier in step two, you need to understand clearly the reasons that persuade clients to buy. These are commonly known as the five main reasons why clients say "Yes" to a purchase. When establishing your USP you should ask yourself how the USP can communicate all of the following reasons for purchase:

1. The desired need:

An interesting definition of a need is that it is a physiological or psychological requirement for the well-being of an organism. In other words; a need can be objective and physical such as food or water, or it can subjective and psychological such as a need for self-esteem. It can be suggested that some physical needs are necessities whereas most psychological needs are actually based on wants and desires. Therefore, the majority of products bought are not purchased with physical needs in mind.

> **ASK YOURSELF**
>
> Why does your client need your product or service?

If your product fails to fall into the physical need category then do not despair. Most clients do not need a new t-shirt, their nails manicured or a state-of-the-art MP3 player, and yet these are still sold in the thousands every day. This is because the marketing surrounding these products may be advertising psychological reasons (benefits) to persuade the client that they need that particular product or service.

2. Emotional connection:

If marketed and packaged correctly, some products or services have the power to have an emotional effect on a client. For example: Kelly is having a bad day. She walks into your clothes shop, sees happy faces and friendly staff who help her find the dress she saw advertised in the window outside. The woman wearing the dress in the advertisement looked happy, confident and stunning. Once she tries the dress on she too feels "like a million dollars".

> ### ASK YOURSELF
>
> How does your product or service make the client feel emotionally?

The whole experience has lifted Kelly's spirits and once again she is in a good mood. The price was a little expensive and she didn't really need the dress (she has many dresses in her wardrobe at home); but that has little effect on her choice to buy the product. The whole pleasant experience of buying the product and the emotional connection she felt when seeing the advertisement, and again when wearing the dress was worth it!

3. Great product:

Some products or services seem to sell themselves. In other words, the clients just love the product or service. The right combination always sells. Maybe, as in the dress scenario the product is the perfect colour or fits like a glove. Or a particular brand was the first to provide their clients with a unique service that proved popular with the clients the first time round, so that generated repeat custom.

> ### ASK YOURSELF
>
> How good is your product in terms of end result compared to your competitors?

4. Loyalty or reward:

Brand loyalty is the client's conscious or unconscious decision, expressed through the behaviour of repurchasing a certain brand, product or service continually. The factor that increases brand loyalty is when the consumer perceives the brand, product or service to offer the right combination of benefits such as: features, image, level of quality and price. Brand loyalty exists because a client's buying behaviour is generally habitual. In other words, clients stick to what they know. Therefore in order to create brand loyalty you may have to break these habits and assist them to acquire new habits. Then reinforce those habits by constantly reminding your clients the benefits of purchasing your products or services.

ASK YOURSELF

 How competitively priced is your product or service?

One method that is commonly used to increase brand loyalty is known as a loyalty programme. These are structured marketing efforts that reward, and therefore encourage loyal buying behaviour. This programme can be referred to in many different terms such as: loyalty card, rewards card, advantage card, discount card or club card. But they all essentially seek the same goal, to persuade the client to return and buy again in exchange for a reward or gain.

5. Price or value:

Price can be a compelling factor in a choice to buy a product as many clients find it difficult to resist a bargain price whether they need the item or not. "I can't miss that at that price!"

However price alone is rarely the deciding factor in choosing to purchase a product and it is certainly not equal to value. Remember generally people do not like cheap. They often prefer value.

Here are a few examples of some of the most well known USP's that you hear on a regular basis. Think about the benefits and the impact that each of these statements have and what impact or desires you have when you read them out:

"You get fresh, hot pizza delivered to your door in 30 minutes or less - or it's free." Domino's Pizza

"When your package absolutely, positively has to get there overnight." FedEx

"The King of Pop" Michael Jackson

"The World's Favourite Airline" British Airways

"It's the real thing" Coca-Cola

"The ultimate driving machine" BMW

"The best a man can get." Gillette

"The milk chocolate melts in your mouth, not in your hand." M&Ms

In summary, the most important thing to remember about a USP is to promote the benefits, not the features. Focus on marketing the "benefits" to your potential clients and what owning or experiencing this product or service brings. The technical/theory's behind your products or service may be great, but your clients are more concerned with the emotional meaning associated with owning it.

Know the Difference Between Price and Value

It is important within business that you know the difference between price and value; as this will ultimately determine on what grounds you sell your products or services. In my World, only once you have identified the difference can you create an effective marketing message powerful enough to capture the client's attention.

In a nutshell, a price is what one must pay to acquire benefits from another party. Most business owners simply use the word price to indicate what it costs to obtain a product. Unfortunately however, most business owners pay little attention to this area and follow suit with their competitors rather than understanding the actual "value" and "price" of their products or services. The decision of pricing is key in business.

> **The only thing that stands between a man and what he wants from life is often merely the will to try it and the faith to believe that it is possible.**
>
> - Richard M. DeVos

Here are a few tips to consider when looking at the price and value of your products and services:

Setting the right price:

Do not set your prices too rapidly based on little or no research and analysis. If you do, then your business could lose out for absolutely no reason. There are three ways that this could happen.

1. If prices are set too high then you may experience resistance from your clients; particularly if your target audience has a low disposable income. Having the price too high could prevent these clients from being able to afford your products.

2. Alternatively, if the prices are set too low then your business may be missing out on those additional profits. This is especially true when your target audience is willing or has a large disposable income to buy your products at the higher prices.

3. Additionally, if the prices are set too high after initial low prices, then your clients may decide that your business is taking advantage of their custom

and so choose to boycott your brand.

Therefore, setting the right price involves invaluable market knowledge, especially with new products.

Price plays a vital part in sales promotion:

In order to stimulate interest in a product you may decide to adjust your price with a short-term sales promotion. However you should also be mindful of running frequent sales promotions. This can lead to your clients anticipating your next reduction in price and consequently waiting until then. Think about furniture stores with regular bi-weekly sales and closing down sales.

Price is most flexible "marketing mix" variable:

Compared to the other marketing decisions like "product", "placing" and "promotion" that can sometimes take months to change; price can be adjusted instantly. This is especially the case when utilizing e-commerce websites and online stores. This flexibility is particularly important when you want to generate interest in certain products or produce increased profits from popular selling products. You could use this as your "trump card" and use it to data capture clients for up-sales once the client has bought into your brand.

Price can often be the trigger of first impressions:

Often as soon as a client learns of the price of a product a perception is made as to the value of that product. For example: If the product is viewed as too cheap then the client may decide that the product is obviously made from "bad" quality materials. Therefore, a client could sometimes actually dismiss a product based on its price alone.

When you set a price on your product or service, it is vital to distinguish between price and value. For most clients price alone is not the deciding factor when they choose to buy a particular product. Typically, most clients will actually compare the package as a whole. These clients will often take into account several different variables before making a choice. The most important of these variables is the value.

> **FACT**
>
> The famous jewellery store Tiffany & Co. was established on September 18, 1837 in New York City. The amount of sales that were made the first day was $4.98.

Value however, is not the same as price. Price is what you pay to receive benefits from an external party. Whereas value is what the buyer believes the benefits of buying the product will actually be. What value (benefits) the buyer obtains from the product is totally dependent on the buyer themselves. For example: The value that a child derives from a bar of chocolate is much greater than what (most) adults would derive. Thus what is valuable to one person may not be valuable to another.

There are in fact many ways in which you can manage how your clients perceive your brand, products or services. Here are some methods you could use:

✓ Offer a free trial or sample of your product. This increases the perceived value because clients believe you have confidence in your product, so it must be good.

✓ Include lots of testimonials in your marketing. This increases the perceived value because you have actual proof of other clients' experiences with your product.

✓ Offer an affiliate program with your product. This increases the perceived value because people can also make money with your product.

✓ Present your clients with a strong guarantee. This increases the perceived value because it again proves that you are confident in the quality of the product.

- ✓ Package your product with many bonuses. This increases the perceived value because people feel they are getting more for their money. For example: Two for the price of one.

- ✓ Get your product endorsed by someone famous. This increases the perceived value because clients think that a celebrity would not want to represent and put their name on a poor product.

- ✓ Create a well-known brand. This increases the perceived value because stereotypically clients believe that a recognized brand name product is better in quality and more reliable.

- ✓ Get your product accredited. If you can show that your product meets certain standards by governing bodies; then this adds creditably to your product and so increases the perceived value.

- ✓ Sell your product at a higher price. This increases the perceived value because clients generally associate the higher price with a higher value.

The reasoning behind these methods is to support the idea that the gain must always outweigh the pain of the gain. If you follow this simple idea then you can almost guarantee that a client will have no reason not to purchase your product.

> **MAGIC FORMULA**
>
> Customer Value = Perceived Value − Perceived Sacrifice

Get Feedback – Testimonials Provide Power!

Clients in general over the years have grown to be very cautious and sceptical of promises advertised within marketing promotions. They therefore generally seek proof or validity of the promises made, and why not? Think about the last time you bought a television. What level of research did you do before actually buying the television? Did you use the Internet to read reviews? Did you compare pixels or perhaps the size?

Now think back to the actual reason why you chose that television over the many thousands available with similar specifications! Did you sit in the store and watch a film to compare the quality? Of course not, it's likely that you received a recommendation from someone else.

In my World, the most common final buying decision is the based upon another's experience of the product or service. Therefore, gathering testimonials is a must for any entrepreneur. Utilizing what others say about your business, product or service is a thousand times more convincing that anything you say, and should be utilized within your marketing efforts. It is obvious that clients will initially doubt what you communicate about your business because you are likely to be biased. However people who are not involved with your business are "neutral", and so have the freedom to speak truthfully about your business, products or services.

> **FACT**
>
> LEGO, is taken from the Danish words "leg godt" which means play well. Or the Latin word which means "play together" but the Danish company say that is just a coincidence.

If you are going to use testimonials, and I would strongly recommend that you do, make sure you choose the testimonials wisely. Whereas some testimonials can prove incredibly powerful; some can actually cause the opposite effect and avert the custom of certain clients. Therefore, it is vital to ensure that your testimonials are strong, convincing ones and are not fabricated.

Here are a few qualities of what makes a strong convincing testimonial:

Make sure testimonials include the specifics:

Vague testimonials always leave room for suspicion. "The service was great" or "Thanks for an excellent product." or "I was very impressed with the services I received at your shop." These statements allow clients to wonder what exactly it was that made the service so great and the product excellent, as a person's perception of "greatness" and "excellence" will vary. Testimonials should promote a certain benefit that would persuade other clients to buy. For example: "I was impressed by the 24 hour reception service at the hotel, and even more so when the receptionist went out of her way to warm my milk for my baby in the hotel kitchen." or "By using X product I started to lose two pounds a week rather than just the pound a week I used to lose before." or "I found the chapter in the book, 'How To Use Testimonials To My Advantage' very useful and have already doubled my product sales worth £10,000!"

> All who have accomplished great things have had a great aim, have fixed their gaze on a goal which was high, one which sometimes seemed impossible.

- Orison Swett Marden

Testimonials must overcome objections:

You will almost undoubtedly come across sceptics about your business, especially if you are new to the market. The trick is to convince these clients and so showcase these cases to other sceptics. Don't be afraid to advertise those testimonials that initially thought badly of your business, and later after testing or experiencing your business, changed their opinion. These testimonials can often be the most powerful!

For example: "I have been in sales for 10 years and thought I knew everything. I attended this course believing that I would not take anything of value away. I thought I was wasting my time. I was very wrong. It turns out that industry has changed and I am now up-to-date with current relevant sales techniques." In order to encourage these sceptics to test or experience your business, products or services in the first place, you may have to offer them a discounted price or in some cases for free. But do not worry, you will see a return. The invaluable testimonials you could potentially receive from these discounted or free trials could be the key in persuading many others to buy into your brand. Consider this type of testimonial as an investment to target like-minded sceptics.

Well-placed within marketing/advertising:

This is particularly relevant on a website. When a client is on your website they could be at different stages of what is known as the buying process. You need to make sure that you have the correct testimonial for the right stage of the client. For example: When a client is in the early stages of buying a product or service they will often come to what is known as a landing page. Be sure that the testimonials on this page are ones that will convince those that may not be ready to "bite".

These testimonials achieve this by answering the questions a perspective client may have such as: How is this going to improve my life? How is this going to work when others have failed? These testimonials sound like this: "I have tried many different products, but my hair still didn't stay in place and it always felt greasy after using the products. But your product held my hair in place all day, and when I brushed my hair later it still felt silky and clean!"

Pages where a client comes later in the buying process such as product pages should provide testimonials that cover any questions the buyer may have regarding the product or service once they are interested in buying. Such as: What happens if I don't like it? Is it the right option for me? These testimonials sound like this: "When I bought my new phone I thought that the £30 talk plan was the right one for me. Later, when using the phone I discovered that I actually used more texts than minutes. So I simply rang the free customer service help line number that came with the phone, and the friendly adviser talked me again through the different options. He quickly updated my plan and I am now saving £10 a month!"

Provide videos or photos of clients giving testimonials:

It is very different reading a testimonial and actually seeing a person saying a testimonial. A video can leave a personal touch and help to prove that the testimonials are real and not fabricated. Be careful to choose clients that are similar to those in your target audience, as they will often relate to the person giving the testimonial. Or on the other hand, you could choose someone that the audience can look to aspire to. Photos are often a great way to demonstrate results. This way of convincing clients is most commonly recognised within the weight-loss industry; with before and after shots. If you can prove the benefits of your product or service in pictures; then it's a great way to boost your sales as it adds the personal touch.

✓ *"Seeing is believing." "A picture paints a thousand words."*

In summary, if you're not using testimonials within your business then you're missing out on one of the most powerful, easy-to-use and cheap marketing tools available. As humans we instantly would prefer to purchase something from a friend than make a purchase based on a sales pitch alone. It's inevitable that your clients, like you, will want to know that the product or services actually works before taking action to buy. It's natural to put more trust in someone who has already used the product successfully than the person trying to convince us to buy it. Using testimonials within your business will let your clients know that you're worthy of their trust.

Ask Your Clients What They Want Next

Business is largely based on your client's wants, needs and requirements. Whereas most businesses attention is focused on creating marketing messages that persuade clients to think they want the products or services they have already provided, entrepreneurs focus their efforts on what the clients are going to buy next!

Promoting the products and services you currently offer is obviously the sensible option to take. While as an entrepreneur you must also consider providing products and services that your clients already know they want, but are not currently available on the market.

It's common knowledge that it is much less time consuming and cheaper to retain current loyal clients than it is to create new ones. This is why it's important allocate some time to periodically ask your existing clients what they want and ensure that you are fulfilling these requirements. During this exercise be sure to encourage your clients to share with you any ideas that may assist your business grow.

ASK YOURSELF

 Are there any other day-to-day problems that occur within your client's life that you may be able to offer a solution to?

 How can you find out what your clients "need" next?

When looking for feedback or ideas from your clients I recommend offering an incentive in exchange for their completed questionnaires and rewarding them with a 5% discount for any improvements that are implemented. This not only invites them to buy into the questionnaire but also to re-purchase.

Here are a few questions that you may want to ask your clients in order to build a better understanding of their future needs. Obviously these would have to be tailored to your specific industry or market.

✓ How did you first find out about us and by what method?

✓ Are there companies that you see as our competitors? If so who?

✓ What was the first reason for seeking this product or service?

✓ When you were shopping and you selected us, what where your initial thoughts?

✓ Did you consider any alternatives businesses? If so, how did you make your decision?

- ✓ Thinking back to when you made your purchase decision, is there anything you saw about us that especially helped you decide to buy from us?

- ✓ Among the companies you mentioned, which one, besides us, would you consider to be the best choice if you were making this decision now?

- ✓ Are there changes about our company that we should make in order to be clearly superior to this competitor?

- ✓ Do you anticipate buying more, or less, or about the same amount next year?

- ✓ Is there something else that you would consider buying from us and what is it?

- ✓ What other sources of information do you consider credible that help you make purchase decisions?

- ✓ What was your thought process leading up to your purchase decision? How long did it take?

- ✓ Did outside advisors (such as consultants, investors) play a role in your decision process?

- ✓ Has our product/service enhanced your profitability or lifestyle needs? If so, how?

- ✓ Are there any additions that would compliment this? (profitability or lifestyle needs)

- ✓ May we use this information within a "testimonial" about our product/service and its value to you on our website and brochures?

After you have established basic rapport using the survey, its then time to ask them ""What do you do?" rather than "What do you need?" Although it seems sensible to ask them what they want, it is very much a different question altogether. Instead of putting them in the role of marketer, trying to get them to do your work for you, what you should be doing is getting them to simply take you through their experience with your product or service.

By asking "What do they do?" your client will give you their experience. Within this context they will tell you what you will need to do to provide a better "value". By listening carefully and asking good questions, you can develop a quality picture of what their experience is and explore ways to improve or redevelop it.

In summary, the more time you dedicate to learning about your clients the better understanding you will have about the direction of your business.

It's Only Got To Be 10% Better Than The Others

As an entrepreneur it's essential that you understand you are not an inventor but a creator. Being highly effective in what you do is what makes you a success. It is therefore better to avoid the need to reinvent the wheel, but think how to make the best opportunities from the "creation" of the wheel.

This misconception or misunderstanding of entrepreneurialism contributes to what I believe is a fundamental stumbling block for many business owners. All too often they get wrapped up within the day-to-day running of their business; and so either forget or miss the opportunity to develop their products and services. To be successful within your business ventures it is important that your mind should always be aware of these areas, and act on them before your competition does.

> ### ASK YOURSELF
>
> Think about your competitor's products and consider how you could improve them by just 10%.

One of my biggest recommendations for achieving the correct attitude as an entrepreneur is to look at everything within your business as being almost complete but never complete; and looking to improve it by just 10%. By doing this you appreciate that development can always be done and attune your mind to achieving excellence and betterment in all areas including sales, design, image and so on. Looking at things this way avoids complacency and fuels a consistent business development.

> **TOP TIPS**
>
> → How could you improve your marketing by just 10%?
>
> → What can be done to increase your brand awareness by just 10%?
>
> → How can you increase your profit by 10% within the next month?
>
> → How can you reduce your outgoings by 10% next month?
>
> → How can you feel emotionally better about your business by 10%?

One of my favourite stories that includes personal belief, desire to achieve and the ability to visualize something better; is the legendary tale of Henry Ford.

Ford had an idea for a new engine involving eight cylinders cast in a single block. He knew that this powerful engine, if put into production, would be a great massive success. He asked his engineers to develop it, and after planning they came back and told him it could not be done. He is quoted to have said: "Produce it anyway." They kept coming back without a workable engine, but he told them to keep trying until they had something. The Ford V8 became one of the most successful engines in history.

In summary, this "10%" improvement can act towards your personal USP that will set you apart from the competition. Remember you only need one strong USP to persuade clients to prefer your product. So in short, just by being a little better, makes a massive difference.

6 - Magical Money

6 Magical Money

What Is Money And Why Do You Want It?

The majority of "people" never really think about what money is and what it means to them. We all think that cash in its physical state is that "green stuff" kept in our wallet or purse; and it is also the stuff we wish we had more of. So many people merely work just to earn money because a typical societal upbringing has led them to believe that they need to work in order to live. "One must go to work to earn enough money in order to afford to buy food or to pay the bills." But is this the only reason that people go to work or earn money? Looking at this in more detail than earlier chapters, you must understand the motives behind your action to achieve monetary abundance.

> **ASK YOURSELF**
>
> → What does money mean to you?
>
> → What motivates you to earn money?
>
> → What is money going to give you?
>
> → What other ways can you achieve finding this?

It is important to understand that money is not simply "money". Money therefore, is not just what the dictionary defines: "A good that acts as a medium of exchange in transactions." It actually represents many things to different people. If money were just money then many people's "money problems" would cease to exist. These people would just work as little as possible and only spend as much as they earned.

Let's be honest, most people always desire more "things". In order to obtain these things generally money needs to be earned. It is therefore not the money that people strive for, it is actually the item bought (by the means of money) that is the objective. But why do we want these "things" in the first place? What do these "things" allow us to do or to have? The simple but ultimate answer is feelings and emotions. Money in my World, simply gives us the means to experience certain feelings or emotions.

> **FACT**
>
> If the entire population of the world is taken as 100, then half of the total wealth would be held by 6 people.

These "feelings" are powerful motivators, especially for entrepreneurs, and is normally what makes us more successful than others. It is important during the early stages of your business to discover which feelings are important to you and why! In discovering this it will also provide an indication as to amount of income you must earn to achieve this. For example: If you decide that stability is your priority (the feeling of being comfortable knowing your bills are paid) then you will most likely earn just enough to live. However, if the feeling of freedom were your priority, then you would need to earn more than what you physically need to live. Freedom could mean being able to go anywhere at any time. In this case it could be to have your own car, yacht or plane. Or it could be having the freedom to eat at any restaurant you choose despite the prices on the menu.

> **TOP TIP**
>
> Learn to respect the fact that not all people have the same reason for obtaining money, over the next few days ask your friends or family why they want money.

When taking this attitude toward money avoid associating money with physical objects. It should be instead connected with the feelings that you receive from the things that money buys. For example: If you want to buy a bigger house, what feelings will you experience once you have accomplished your goal of earning enough money to buy that house? Is this a sense of achievement, success or pride? Does everyone else in your family have better things than you do and you want to feel that you fit in? Or is your college reunion coming up soon and you wanted to feel a sense of self-worth when you show off your new house?

According to sociology researchers, humans are motivated by personal goals and physical needs. However personal goals only become significant once a physical need is satisfied. For example: The personal goal of buying a new laptop is seen as unimportant if you can't already afford to buy food for the week. This concept is best described within Maslow's hierarchy of needs. In his paper *A Theory of Human Motivation*, Maslow presents five clear stages of needs in the shape of a pyramid. The idea Maslow demonstrated with the shape of the pyramid was that a person would only move onto the next step once the layer below was satisfied.

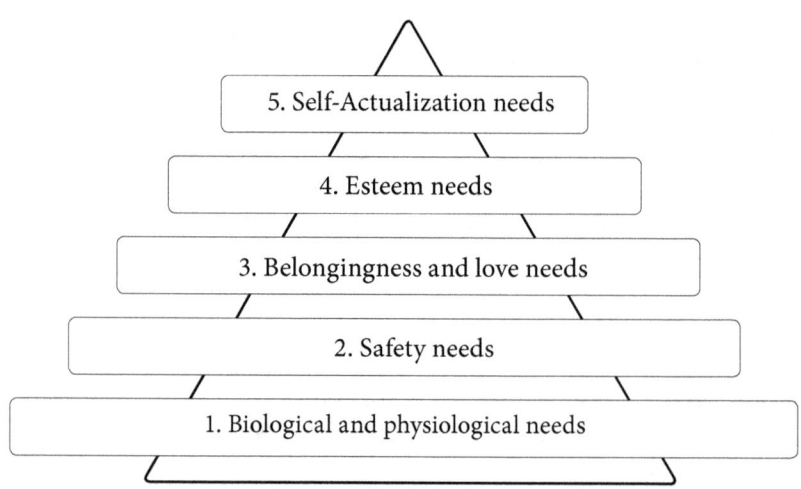

Although I completely agree with Maslow's theory, and utilize this within my life, I think it can be taken to the next level especially within business community. In my World, I believe that the pyramid should not be a pyramid but should be a lateral line, similar to that of a timeline. This would mean that you can have one or more of the five needs in any hierarchy including segments, if you choose. Obviously it is important to have the biological and physiological needs, but fulfilment within one of the others can actually be achieved in the order that best suits your legacy, rather than what is deemed to be needed!

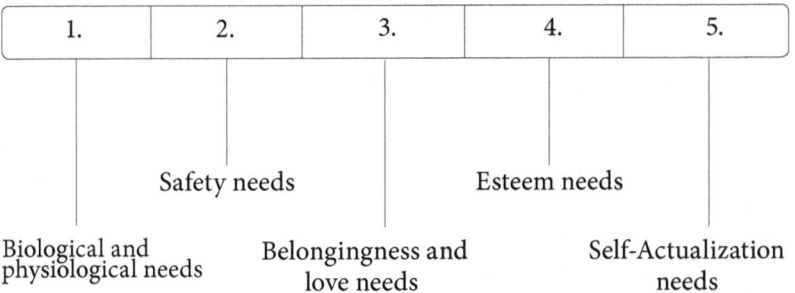

As yourself what order would you put these needs in hierarchy of importance:

✓ Air, food, water, shelter, warmth
✓ Protection from elements, security, order, stability
✓ Work group, family, affection
✓ Self-esteem, achievement, status, independence
✓ Self-Actualization needs – realizing personal potential, self-fulfilment

A top tip is to take the time during your allocated monthly business planning and think about the reasons why you want to reach a certain income level and what it means to you at that specific stage within your business. This answer will change with time; therefore it is important to establish where you are within this thought process. Here are some ideas to get you started:

✓ Do you want the power and prestige that comes along with being a high earning entrepreneur?
✓ Do you want more flexibility with your time?
✓ Do you want a more stable future?

✓ Do you want to travel? Pay off bills? Feel safe and secure?

Remember, it should never be the actual money that you really want, but what the feelings associated with having this money for buying the things you want. When you uncover what those feelings are and how they affect you, then you will know what motivates you to earn money. Without knowing your driving force, you will never fully achieve your goals.

Selling At A Profit Is Easy When You Have The Internet!

When you think about marketing a new product, the actual cost of marketing has to be taken into consideration. The cost normally involved can be exorbitant, but it doesn't need to be if you have access to the Internet. Typically, most business owners in order to meet the massive expense of advertising, are required to either reduce the amount of profit they retain on each item sold or increase the overall price presented to the client. For example: Running a full-page ad in a magazine or a three-minute commercial can often prove very costly, especially for new or small businesses. Consequently, most marketing budgets are set high.

> " Make no small plans for they have not the power to stir men's blood. "
>
> - Niccolo Machiavelli

While traditional methods of marketing also offer some means of reaching its target audience, the opportunity created by Internet marketing has grown to be the most popular marketing medium. With many savvy entrepreneurs aggressively using search engine optimization and other techniques to quickly get in touch with remote consumers. Why?

Well, there are several advantages of using the Internet that you should consider to when marketing your products or services. Listed here are just a few that I consider to be the most beneficial:

Much larger audience for a cheaper price:

Internet marketing is relatively inexpensive when compared to the ratio of cost against the reach of the target audience. In other words, compared to other forms of marketing, Internet marketing has the potential to contact a far greater (in numbers) audience making the cost per person much smaller. If you think about the number of people who have access to the Internet compared to the number of people that read your local paper.

It can be instant with no delays:

When placing an ad in a local newspaper there are a few time constraints before your advert is even viewed by your audience. This is known as lead-time and includes the time taken to process, print and distribute the newspaper. Consequently, you could be left waiting anywhere from a couple of days to sometimes weeks depending on the publication to see any return on your investment. The Internet however is instant. Once your post or advert is uploaded it can be viewed immediately. There is therefore no delay in seeing the results as sales can occur within seconds of the ad being posted.

The Internet is not geographically restricted:

The Internet is not local or nationwide, it is worldwide – hence the appropriate name of the World Wide Web. Unlike the billboard that most probably will only be seen by those who live locally or those who are visiting the area, an Internet advert can be viewed by anyone in the world. The Internet has given smaller businesses the opportunity to market to a global audience, and therefore grow into much larger international businesses.

Long lifespan - you get more for your money:

The turnaround of most marketing methods is relatively short. Magazines are the best example of this as some are released once or twice a week. Once a magazine is read and has outlived its purpose it is usually thrown away or put to the bottom of a pile. After uploading a post or advert to the Internet however, it is displayed indefinitely. Or until you decide when it must be updated or removed.

"Nothing is particularly hard if you divide it into small jobs."

- Henry Ford

Any adverts can be instantly measurable:

The effectiveness of Internet marketing can be tracked, measured and tested. In other words, each time a particular advert is clicked on or an article is read, it is recorded. Every action the client makes is noted and is free to access, thanks to certain software. An entrepreneur is now able to see exactly how many clients viewed their posts, pages, and adverts and so on to determine what and where to place more material. All this is not possible with other forms of marketing. With billboards it is impossible to know exactly how many people viewed the advert.

It can cut out manufacturing and so increase the profit per product:

With the introduction and increase of the digital era there is in some cases no need for physical products. "Downloads" essentially, cut out manufacturing time and costs and so overall profits received are increased. For example: Music in particular can now be purchased as an MP3 that is transferred directly onto an MP3 player, with no need of an actual physical CD. The same can be said for e-books that can be read via laptops, Amazon's Kindle or now Apple's iPad, with no need to incur printing costs.

The increasing popularity of the Internet:

Increasingly, most clients would agree that their search for products or services initially begins with the Internet. Even for the simplest items or products/services (that could even be found in their local area) most clients will still opt to look online. But why is this? It is less time consuming. The client is able to find exactly what they are looking for online by the use of search engines. It is more convenient. "Internet shopping" is available 24 hours, 7 days a week and the client doesn't even have to get dressed!

Auction/e-commerce websites:

The best example of this is the online auction marketplace known as eBay. Many small businesses have only been able to exist with the use of eBay. EBay enables entrepreneurs to start their business fully online and immediately reach a market of millions of registered users worldwide. Therefore eBay is increasingly becoming the best place to start, grow and operate a small business.

ASK YOURSELF

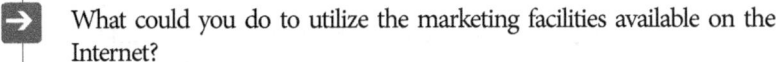 What could you do to utilize the marketing facilities available on the Internet?

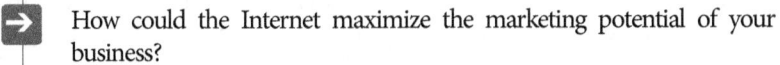 How could the Internet maximize the marketing potential of your business?

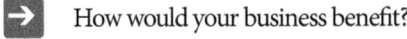 How would your business benefit?

In summary, utilizing the web tools available, web marketing helps businesses expand from just being in a local market, to a national or international level, in a much faster way. When this method is compared to other types of traditional media like radio, print or television; online marketing does have an advantage when it comes to low start-up costs and cost per client ratio.

Clients That Pay Late vs. Clients Who Pay On Time!

In my World, there is nothing more frustrating than delivering your products or services on time, only to have to deal with a client that pays late or just doesn't pay at all. Slow and late paying clients drain your business resources and are most defiantly a major source of frustration. Bad clients can waste extensive amounts of time requiring multiple collection calls and reminders in order to finally pay. From experience slow paying clients can create significant problems within your business, especially if your cash flow is tight or re-investing profits. As an entrepreneur the rule is simple; you must look after those who look after you.

ASK YOURSELF

 What are the most common reasons why your clients fail to pay on time?

 How can this be identified earlier on during the business relationship?

 What systems could you implement to ensure this doesn't happen?

Business owners are naturally passionate about their money and why not, their business and future custom depends on it. However when cash is tight, they can fall into the trap of going into a negative state; which I call the "collections" mode. These business owners will try every conceivable way to get late paying clients to pay up, and as a result become completely unaware of the adverse effects it's having. This is an understandable knee-jerk reaction to a tough problem. Unfortunately, it seldom works and the effort lost outweighs the profit gained. It's inevitable that late clients will keep paying late. If you feel the need to pursue bad payers yourself, then avoid forgetting about good paying clients, as they will get upset by the collections tactics. This ends up being a lose-lose situation for all involved.

As an entrepreneur you will have to ensure that your fear of upsetting bad payers is left behind and only encourage reliable buyers; those who are good to their word and pay on time. Within your business ventures it's inevitable that you will experience different types of buyers. Outlined here are some of the ones you may want to avoid:

Looking but not buying - these are not serious buyers but will waste your time:

Humans are generally very curious, it's in our nature. We are naturally drawn to changes in our environment, especially if these changes are accompanied by flurries of activity. These clients are therefore just inquiring and so are not serious about buying your product or service.

Unqualified buyers – they do not have the means to fund the product or service:

It is very difficult to quickly access whether a client is financially viable to afford your product or service. This is because most clients are never too eager to share their financial history and because appearances can be deceiving. If eventually you discover that your client is unqualified; then you would have wasted precious time that could have been spent on a more qualified buyer.

Bargain hunters – the clients who look for low prices:

This type of client is not looking to pay over the odds for your products or services despite any added value you may have attempted to attach. These clients are typically driven by what they can get for their money. Therefore they look for low prices that they can bargain even lower.

Wheeler-dealers – these clients want to buy in order to sell on and make a profit:

Again this type of client is looking for low prices. This buyer is only motivated to buy if they believe that the price they pay leaves room for them to make a "tidy profit".

So how do you avoid these types of buyers? There are several methods that you can utilize to ensure you deter these types of clients and so instead attract qualified, serious and motivated clients that pay on time.

Raise your prices:

As most of the "time wasting" clients are driven by low prices you can quickly discourage these clients by raising your prices alone.

Pay-up-front:

This eliminates any doubts you may have about an unreliable client as the payment is received before the client obtains their product or service. A pay-up-front method usually involves the full amount owed. Because of this the situation is reversed and it is the client that is taking all of the risk. For instance, how can the client be sure that you are good to your word? Therefore, using this method may discourage some clients.

Deposit:

In order to overcome the problems found using the pay-up-front method you may want to use the deposit method whereby the risk is divided between the parties. A deposit is an amount of money to show intention to complete the purchase of the product or service. This method could be described as a meeting half-way point. For example: The client initially pays half, therefore demonstrating to the seller that they are reliable before receiving the product or service. Later the client completes payment if the seller has proven reliable on the product or service.

Set terms & conditions – contract:

When outlining your terms & conditions before a transaction takes place you ensure that your clients understand clearly their role in the contract or "deal". Once signed or agreed to by the client this can act as a legal document if complications arise. Clients are left with no excuse to follow through everything that they have signed or agreed to, and are therefore more motivated. This is especially important if the transaction requires payment in installments. The client needs to understand the dates that payment is due and how much this is likely to cost. Do not deviate from your terms if someone doesn't pay within your set period, you may need to send a reminder letter. Late payments are in effect resisting the growth of your business and jeopardizing future service to clients. Do not be fearful about instructing your legal professional to chase money on your behalf.

In summary, there are many ways to ensure that you receive the money entitled to you, but do not fall into the trap of desperately seeking the next order at any cost. Protect your business and choose your clients wisely. Even if requiring a deposit or contact drives off a few potential clients, it's worth the saved collection headaches. Pass all collection responsibilities onto your legal professional and focus on the development of your business.

Up-Selling And Cross-Selling - Good And Bad Practices

In my World, entrepreneurs should always be looking for the best way to maximise the profit from each client. If you are familiar with sales techniques then it is likely that you would have come across the terms "up-selling" and "cross-selling". If you aren't then it's an area that can massively increase your businesses income. Up-selling refers to when a business induces a client to purchase a more expensive item, upgrade or add-on, in an attempt to make a more profitable sale. Cross-selling on the other hand refers to when a business attempts to sell something else after a client has committed to purchasing the first product.

ASK YOURSELF

→ What products do you have that could complement each of your sales?

→ How much extra revenue would this generate if it was sold to just 30% of your clients?

→ What could you do to implement this?

Both up-selling and cross-selling can prove to be very profitable parts of your business. Think about this for a moment: If you sold a car with monthly payments of £400 with an add-on of £5 per month charged for upholstery protection. After 12 months of payments, it creates the sum of £60. Multiplied by 50 car sales a month, creates an additional yearly sum of £3,000. While it may initially seem that this return is very little; put into context this up-sell may only have taken as little as two minutes to conduct therefore making it overall, a pretty worthwhile investment of time.

Consequently, learning to up-sell and cross-sell is vitally important because it allows you to create more revenue streams from existing clients. This is particularly vital as maintaining an existing client is less expensive and time consuming than creating a new lead. It should be understood however, that not all up-selling and cross-selling techniques work. There are in fact good and bad practices of these techniques. It is therefore vital that you learn the factors that determine whether up-selling and cross-selling is effective within your business. Here are a few of those factors:

Avoiding up-selling or cross-selling:

Obviously, if you purposely miss opportunities to up-sell or cross-sell then it is clear that you will not see the benefits of using these techniques. You should never be afraid to use these processes as, if they are done correctly, the client is actually more satisfied. This is largely because they are persuaded to believe that they are getting the better deal. However, make sure you are confident that the product or service you are up-selling adds value to the original product or service. If it doesn't then do not continue with the sale.

Always have a "favourite" up-sale:

Some entrepreneurs involved within the sales industry have typical "favourites" that they have up-sold or cross-sold many times previously. This is largely because they are well prepared or versed in pitching the advantages of this "favourite" product or service to the client. This ensures that the up-sell or cross-sell does not appear fake or unreliable to the client.

Become aware of your client's background and budget:

Becoming aware of your client's background and budget as you talk to them allows you to choose the appropriate product to up-sell or cross-sell. This correct choice will therefore reduce the chances of the client refusing that product or service. Know what your client "actually" wants and fulfill the need.

Don't be too arrogant or too pushy:

As mentioned previously, when practicing sales techniques in general you must not be too forceful. Again you must become a client's trusted consultant rather than just a salesperson whose only concern is to make a profit.

Show or demonstrate the physical product:

"Seeing is believing." If you can present your client with the actual physical product, then this may persuade the client to buy. Holding, touching, and smelling are all ways in which a client interacts with a physical product. Therefore, if a client can experience this before buying, then it may be the deciding factor.

A flowing afterthought and not another sales pitch:

The most effective way to transform a closing sale into an up-sell or cross-sell is in a very "by the way" kind of manner. It should sound like an afterthought and not just another sales pitch. An example of this would be: "Actually, we offer something else that will really help you out…"

> ❝ Winners are those people who make a habit of doing the things losers are uncomfortable doing. ❞
>
> - Ed Foreman

In a nutshell, if you are too forceful then a client may start to think that you are wasting their time by selling products or services that they don't actually need. Remember you must always go for a win-win situation. In other words both you as the seller and the client should "win" from the exchange. A "deal" must never end in a lose on your side and a win on the clients or vice versa.

Still Keep the Door Open Even If There's A Draft

In every business there will be times when you may reach a comfortable state. In other words profits are decent enough so why spend more time and money on marketing? However, you may have heard the saying: "It's either feast or famine." This statement can prove very true especially in terms of business affairs. During those times of "feasting," where industry is booming and profits are plentiful; remember that "famine" could be just around the corner. Here are a few ways that your business can survive a time of "famine" or hard times, particularly in terms of marketing.

Ensure your client base is economically spread:

It is important to understand that you cannot depend on only one target group of clients. Industry is forever changing and this also has an effect on your clients. For example: Your business markets holidays abroad to low-income families. The government decides to lower the amount families receive in benefits such as working tax credit and child benefits.

Your target audience are now unable to afford your holidays abroad and are opting for much more local short breaks. If however, you had marketed your holidays to young professionals (who are not affected by the decrease in benefits), then you would still have profits being generated out of this audience.

Take advantage of the times of abundance and maintain marketing efforts to potentially increase your client base. The more varied your clients, then the less effect certain changes will have on your profits.

Don't avoid marketing to those who only buy little or irregularly:

There are some clients who, when purchasing products or services from you, don't particularly buy or spend a lot. You may therefore feel that marketing efforts concentrated on this audience is of little value. However, these clients may still have the potential to become loyal clients and so return. Loyal clients are of high value because they are more likely to return and keep spending despite any industry changes.

Don't ever stop marketing:

The phone is ringing off the hook. Your inbox is overflowing. Your staff complain that they have little time off and you cry: "I don't have time to market; my business has enough business already. There is no way I could cope with more!"

If you are overwhelmed with business then it may be tempting to put a freeze on your promotions. But how can you be certain that this influx is going to last? Capitalize on times of thriving industries and this can later fund the times when industry deteriorates. Also use these times as an excuse to streamline the operations of your business. For example: This could be cutting production times in order to meet demands. Make sure your marketing continues when times are abundant.

ASK YOURSELF

→ What can you do you ensure that your business never stops marketing?

→ How far in advance can you schedule promotional offers to existing clients?

→ How can this be done without utilizing a massive resource of time or money?

So the solution is; no matter how much or how well you think you've made your point, there's always room for something more or something new to keep your product or service in the minds of potential clients. So even if your product is arguably the best in the World, there's always some reason to keep getting your message out there.

7 - Marketing & Advertising

7 Marketing & Advertising

The Right Image – Professional, Poor or Peasant

When projecting the image of a business to their clients, many business owners incorrectly assume what they like, their clients will like. In my World, it doesn't matter what you, yourself think is acceptable, it is actually what the clients perceive that is significant. As an entrepreneur, you will need to put much consideration into how your clients see your business in its current state, and how this differs from what you would like them to think of your business. If that means a "trusted consultant", then you may need to make the necessary changes in order to communicate this message to your audience.

ASK YOURSELF

 Is your business being presented in the best possible way?

 What image comes to mind when looking at your branding?

 How could this be better?

It is important to understand that in theory there is not a right or wrong answer to creating the correct "image". This is largely determined by an individual's opinion and obviously varies from one client to the next. Despite this, there are a few recommendations and things to avoid that are agreed by the majority when portraying your business to your clients.

Avoid appearing desperate for business:

I have witnessed many businesses that have amazing products and services, yet they give the appearance of being desperate for business. This is not good! Desperation can give off negative vibes and so creates discouraging feelings that can contribute to an unwanted overall negative buying experience. I often refer to this desperate approach as a "poor or peasant attitude". If a business is managed with this negative attitude then this "negativity" will eventually be transferred onto the clients. So leaving room for the clients to doubt the business. In other words, if a client believes that a business is about to close down, then they may then feel that there must be something wrong with the product or service because few people are buying it!

> **FACT**
>
> People in the USA get so hyper about the Super Bowl that the sale of antacids increases by 20% every year after the day of the game.

To avoid giving off this kind of image you may need to take inspiration from this common saying: "fake it until you make it". In other words, you must create a convincing persona that your business is successful even if it isn't. You shouldn't lie, or deceive but create a professional image that could be perceived as a large enterprise or a small independent. Once your client "thinks" that a business is doing well "their opinion" of that business becomes more positive. A client is then encouraged to think: "Well the product must be good because the business looks as if it is doing well; which suggests that lots of people are buying the product." This simple tool can radically change the clients that you attract and the confidence you have in representing your business.

Avoid transferring your negativity onto a client:

Obviously in business it is important to be honest with your clients. However if I am honest, this strictly speaking is not always the case! It is important to note that your clients do not want to be burdened with your own personal issues or any negative opinions you may have of your business. One of the main reasons why clients buy products or services is to gain emotions, and these particular emotions are always positive. Clients do not want a negative buying experience. If you are having issues in your personal life, then deal with them and leave them at the office door. Taking personal issues to work creates a state of resentment towards your work and produces negativity.

"A good plan today is better than a great plan tomorrow."

- General George S. Patton

Avoid over promising to yourself or to your clients:

It is important in business never to over promise especially if this promise appears unfeasible. If a client has any doubt that your statements are not physically viable and as a result, do not believe them, then your client will develop an overall negative opinion about your business. Clients will not want to buy from a business they believe to be untrustworthy or untruthful. Be 100% honest with yourself and your clients, and this will naturally be projected through your marketing message.

> **ASK YOURSELF**
>
> What do you currently promise to your clients?
>
> How do you know that you are delivering this effectively?

Present professional looking integrated marketing material:

Many business owners start out on a shoestring budget when it comes to marketing and advertising. However, it is very important that any printed marketing material that you put out for the public to see doesn't say "budget" or "cheap". Remember, you are competing against dozens, if not hundreds of other businesses in your area or in the case of the Internet, globally. A simple black-and-white flyer is not going to stand up against a glossy oversized postcard, or professionally designed Internet banners when it comes to attracting a client's interest. Spend your marketing budget wisely, making sure that the materials you put out are professional and to a high standard. Also make sure that your marketing messages are integrated especially during a campaign. By that I mean that all of them are communicating an identical message. Avoid releasing adverts that contradict each other, as again this will damage your client's perception of your business.

> **FACT**
>
> A Tupperware party starts somewhere in the world every 23 seconds.

Brand your business well:

Although we touched on this during Chapter One, too many businesses fail to brand themselves in the beginning, when it is most needed. When you are deciding on your company name and business idea, it is a good idea to also consider how you want your clients to remember you. This means that you may want to come up with a logo, mascot or tagline that will allow the public to know exactly who you are and remember your name. You might even want to invest in a vanity phone number that will help clients remember how to call you easily and quickly. You want clients thinking that: "There is no need to look up their phone number because they have branded themselves in such a way that it is easy to remember how to get in contact." Spend some money at the beginning on creating on a brand that you would be proud to represent your business. If in doubt get a professional to do it for you.

Make your business attractive:

When running advertising campaigns, it's a good idea to ensure your adverts are attractive to your clients. You will need to know the types of words and styles of design that generate a response from your target audience, and so utilize these in your marketing material.

> **ASK YOURSELF**
>
> Where does the image of your business fit in with your competitors?

If you are selling fishing equipment (target market: males between 30 and 60) then you're going to have to make your marketing attractive to this type of client. If you are "female only" selling gym memberships; then again your marketing is going to have to be attractive to that type of client. You need to grasp early on that clients can quickly ignore your marketing efforts if they don't resonate with them.

In terms of the style of the design, this is largely determined by what you discover during your client research. Always refer back to your business plan if needed, and avoid second guessing. Another general way of making sure your marketing material is attractive is to communicate a message that is not overcomplicated or cryptic. Clients will instantly get bored if they have to search to reveal your advertised message.

Mission Statement – Creating Your Final Legacy

Your business like life, is in my opinion only restricted by time, and therefore has something which I call a timeline. In simple terms your business is born, then grows and later it "can" providing you want it to, have an end. Because of this, I believe a mission statement is an absolute must for every business. However rather than using the word mission I prefer to use the word legacy (missions can be completed where as a legacy lasts forever).

> **FACT**
>
> The Mall, the biggest departmental store in Washington, D. C. is 1.4 times bigger than the Vatican City.

You've probably heard the term legacy (mission) statement many times within personal development books, motivational MP3 or any form of self-help resources. While some unlucky business owners think it's a waste of time to create one, I actually believe that a legacy statement can be used as a vital tool in understanding the overall plan and direction of your business. This is because the definition of a legacy statement is a formal, written statement of the fundamental purpose of your business and so answers the question:

"Why do we exist?" Predominantly, it provides a guide and framework on which every decision for the business is made. So any idea that conflicts with your legacy statement should be avoided or discarded. The reason for this is that a legacy statement can act as a strong set of business values, and of course, as an entrepreneur your "values are the priority".

> **Do not wait; the time will never be 'just right'. Start where you stand, and work with whatever tools you may have at your command, and better tools will be found as you go along.**
>
> - Napoleon Hill

Your legacy statement may include any number of factors including the aim and purpose of your business or the products and services your business offers. However it should state what distinguishes the business from its competition and more importantly communicate the business's core ideology and visionary goals. You must also ensure that your legacy statement is clear and concise so that there is no uncertainty as to the direction of the business.

A business legacy statement should:

✓ Define what the business is.

✓ Define what the business aspires to be or achieve.

✓ Distinguish the business from its competition.

✓ Serve as a framework to evaluate current activities.

✓ Be broad enough to allow for creative growth.

✓ Stated clearly so that it's understood by all.

ASK YOURSELF

→ What do you want to be known for and how can this be incorporated within your legacy statement?

→ What do you aim to achieve in the "end" of your time within your business?

→ How would you like your business to be remembered 100 years from now?

Also you may also want to include:

The moral/ethical position of the enterprise, the desired public image, a description of the target market, a description of the products or services the business offers as well as expectations of the growth and profitability.

A great legacy statement is the one used by the Preamble to the Constitution of the United States: "We the people of the United States, in order to form a more perfect union, establish justice, insure domestic tranquillity, provide for the common defence, promote general welfare, and secure the blessings of liberty to ourselves and our posterity, do ordain and establish this Constitution of the United States."

Remember that your legacy statement is likely to survive a lot longer than you or your current clients. When you eventually arrive at the day when it is time to close your business, hand your legacy statement down to your heir or even sell it off; you should be able to look at your legacy statement and know that you personally created that proud statement and that it will live on.

Attention Interest Desire Action – Stop and Think

A common term used in communication and marketing is A.I.D.A. This is a short acronym that was devised as a reminder of the four stages of the sales process. A.I.D.A stands for Attention, Interest, Desire and Action. Without understanding this concept, it is almost impossible to create an advertising or marketing campaign that will be profitable. This is because this concept covers the key areas for the deliverance of an effective message.

There have been many studies that claim roughly how many commercial messages the public are exposed to every day. Confusingly each of these studies declare a whole host of different numbers. Despite this dispute, it is universally agreed that not all of these commercial messages produce a response from their intended audience and so many go unnoticed. To demonstrate this, you could actively look out for those advertising messages during your next journey to work. Make a mental note of all of the ones you never noticed before and I am certain you will be surprised as how many there actually are.

Once you have noticed how many messages you previously ignored; you can then start to critically look at the reasons why this was. Begin to question why those previously unnoticed adverts failed to grab your attention. What is the difference between the adverts you were aware of and the ones that slipped under your radar? The answer will always come back to the theory of A.I.D.A. The effective adverts have been strategically designed, placed and structured in such a way as to grab attention, generate interest, invoke desire and therefore cause action. These adverts have not been thrown together in five minutes and sent out for the public. They are instead well-planned and thought-out tactics.

As an entrepreneur, you must learn how to use the A.I.D.A approach in order to ensure that your marketing efforts are effective. I have previously mentioned that advertising does not come cheap. It is more cost effective to ensure that those adverts you do pay for generate the best possible results.

The A.I.D.A theory in detail:

Attention:

Firstly, you need to get a client's attention. Without their attention it is impossible to convince them of anything and so your message would go unnoticed. It has been estimated that you have a three-second window in which to capture your client's attention in order to persuade them that your message is worthy of their time and so read on. This is largely because if a client took the time to read every marketing message that was presented to them; then there would be little time in their day for anything else. As a result of this a client can afford to be picky about the ones that they do choose to spend their time engaged with.

> **FACT**
>
> Andrew Carnegie – Founder of the Carnegie Steel Company. When adjusted, his net worth lies somewhere between $75 billion to $298 billion.

There are many ways in which to grab a client's attention; but I am only going to explain in detail one in particular as this is the most commonly used. This is the method of using a headline, but as with anything, there are good and bad examples.

✓ John Parker (It's your business name but what do you do?).

✓ John Parker Gyms (Now I know what you do but so what?).

✓ Do you want to get fitter? (Better, now I know the problem).

✓ 5 ways to get fit quickly! (Great, now I know the problem and the solution!).

✓ How business owners can still get fit during their busy lifestyle! (Fantastic, now I know you are talking about me, my problem and how I can resolve it!)

As demonstrated here, the first headline is vague and failed to initially grab attention. Working through to the last statement, this one captures the attention; but also works to withhold crucial information that causes the client to be intrigued to discover.

Interest:

Once you have captured your client's initial attention, you then have the task of ensuring you sustain this attention with the use of interest. The more interested a client is in your advert, the more time you have to communicate your full message. Obviously the more of the message you communicate the greater the chances of that message being effective. Ideally, the message being communicated should be as short and concise as possible, as this task of maintaining attention can be tough. It is also important at this stage to avoid any possibility of your clients becoming bored, because as soon as boredom occurs their attention is again lost. Unfortunately, there have been reports that clients are becoming accustomed to advertising. So businesses are being forced to take more creative approaches to advertising to avoid this client boredom or even to catch their attention in the first place.

> **"Making the simple complicated is commonplace; making the complicated simple, awesomely simple, that's creative."**
>
> - Charles Mingus

Desire:

There is a big difference between a need and a desire; I touched on this subject in previous chapters. Even if a client recognizes they have a need this is not always a stronger motivator than having a desire. By creating a desire for your product or service you are essentially prompting your client to act. One method used to generate more desire for a product or service is to communicate its limitability: "Limited Edition: Only 500 Available In The World, Take Advantage Now!"

Action:

This is the stage when a client commits to taking the action necessary to purchase your product or service. Therefore, make sure that when a client reaches this stage your marketing message includes those essential details that they require to obtain your product or service. For example a phone number, e-mail address, website address or even directions to your business. Regardless of arriving at this stage, a client can still forget contact details if they decide to act at a later date. So in order to ensure that this action is completed instantly you could offer an incentive: "The First 100 People Who Take Action Today Receive A Massive 50% Discount!"

> **TOP TIP**
>
> On average, people can only remember between seven plus or minus two pieces of information consciously at any one time (ask your colleague to close their eyes and name you 10 things around the room without pausing).

Using the A.I.D.A formula will help you ensure that any kind of marketing, whose purpose is to get the reader to do something, is as effective as possible. Remember it must first grab the target audience's attention, and engage their interest. Then it must build a desire for the product offering, before setting out how to take the action that you want the audience to take.

Stop Paying, Start Blogging – Website Essentials

Blogging has changed the dynamics of the Internet and how web savvy entrepreneurs operate. A blog is simply a running commentary of descriptions, events, articles and images that can be delivered on a near instant basis. Although first used back in the 1990's, thanks to sites such as "twitter," business owners are only now discovering the power of "blogging" to massively aid their marketing efforts. As a result blogs are beginning to become an essential tool in any marketing strategy; and a "must" for you if you are looking to build your business in line with growing trends and website optimization.

Due to the popularity of the Internet over the last decade, business owners have, on occasion been faced with the choice of investing money in the latest technology trends. Unfortunately those who failed to follow the growing trends of modern technology and client demands were left behind. Many suffered as a devastating result of this choice. Due to the popularity of "blogging" business owners are now presented with the option to incorporate blogs into their original website and keep their clients updated with the latest news and information regarding their industry.

Outlined below are some of the advantages of utilizing blogging as a means of communication:

As blogs are updated on a more regular basis search engines such as Google, Yahoo and Ask.com prefer these, and often rank these "blogs" much higher within searches. Adding regular content is proven to be much better for optimization than static websites that rarely change. Standard "static" websites are commonly built by a web designer. The information on these websites is (in most occasions) only updated at the build stage with basic information about services, products, provided by the business. Unless of course you have access to a back end user system and change the content yourself. Before you invest large amounts of money in this type of website I would recommend comparing the functionality with blog themed websites, as from experience changing your mind later can be a costly choice.

> **FACT**
>
> As of 2009, an estimated quarter of Earth's population use the services of the Internet.

Blogs offer a mass of advantages to the smaller business or entrepreneur and can be built quickly with the use of free software and templates. These blog based facilities and are easy to access and update by people who know little or nothing about web design.

The major advantage is that you won't need a master's degree to get started. In fact your blog can be built with certain systems within 10 clicks. When thinking about it like this, you'll start to understand that utilizing blogs to market your products and services is relatively inexpensive when compared to most other marketing vehicles such as TV, billboards, and magazines.

In the eyes of your clients, by constantly updating the information held within your website/blog gives them a reason to constantly revisit and see something new. As well as this, there is the option to read other client's comments and even make a comment themselves. This interactivity generates interest around the products or services that are continually being discussed. One of the advantages of this commenting function is that a business owner can actually control the direction of these comments. For example any negative comments or spam can be removed, and the clients who posted the comment can be contacted and any issues resolved.

> **TOP TIP**
>
> "Google – "website optimization tips" and see what the professionals have to say. Do not fall into the trap of believing that an external agency can get you to the top of search engines within weeks. Often this process can take months, unless you of course you use an effective blog based website.

As mentioned earlier, it is important to receive feedback from your clients and this is a fantastic tool to do so. By referring back to the feedback given within these blog articles you can predominantly improve and develop your products and services and ensure your clients are satisfied. You may even want to test the reaction of the market by writing a blog that talks about a new product you want to release.

If you are wondering what to "blog" about then here are a few ideas:

Imagine for a moment that you owned a Golf Pro Shop called "Discount Golf Pro Centre". Within this store you offer wholesale golf equipment at discounted prices. Your web team recently incorporated a blog into your existing website after you heard that it was the latest thing to keep clients revisiting your website; and a great way to get higher on search engines. After talking with various clients about what they would like to see written on this blog page, they simply said: *"Anything to make my game better."* That night after a busy day at work you sit down and start to tap away. Within minutes you have completed your first article titled: "How To Choose The Best Golf Clubs." The next day you cut and paste the title into your search engine and notice that you are on the front page. You also check your website stats and notice that overnight your webpage visitors increased by 50% and online sales increased by 3%. That night you write another: "Top Tips For Chipping Onto The Green", the same happens the following day and so on. Suddenly you capture a massive online client list and increase your profits simply based on your blog articles.

FACT

 Dr. Lieven P. Van Neste owns more than 200,000 domain names.

Although it seems a fairly simplistic way of generating new business, this is a prime example of how powerful sharing your industry knowledge can be. It is also advisable to "blog" around your subject even if the subject isn't directly related to your business, as the aim is to capture as many clients as you possibly can. So in the example of the "Golf Pro Shop" blog titles could include: "The Best Courses To Play For Beginners", How To Grow Putting Grass In Your Garden", "How To Get On The U.S Open" and "What Is The Best Time To Tee Off?"

ASK YOURSELF

 How long would it take for you to write a 200 word article and post it on your blog daily?

 What advice could you provide your clients?

 What new products could you talk about?

By doing this you will increase the traffic you can draw to your website, and the more you will improve page rankings on search engine websites. High ranking on a search engine website is crucial because most clients when browsing the Internet will use a search engine to find what they are looking for. Very rarely will they click into the third or later page of listings, despite the search engine bringing back 200,000 or more results!

> **ASK YOURSELF**
>
> When was the last time you clicked on the 2nd, 3rd or even last page on search engines?

It goes without saying that your blog will need to be constantly updated. So schedule in time to post at least one blog per day, every day! Remember, the more blogs you post the more reasons you give your clients to visit your site. Ultimately, the more traffic you again draw to your business website. In effect the act of "Blogging" can be viewed as a numbers game, the more you blog the more visitors and the more chances of online sales.

If you can get the hang of the blogging lifestyle, you will find that your marketing and advertising costs will go down dramatically. Most people utilize the Internet looking for businesses before they ever turn to phone directories or visiting stores. By being online and having good information that people can use, you will be right there at their fingertips. This will in turn create better brand recognition.

PR- Adding Value To Your Market

Public relations (PR), is a very misunderstood topic for many business owners and as a result is often discarded. However, in my business, free publicity is one of the most effective ways to promote business; and doesn't affect the marketing budget. Appearing regularly in the newspapers, magazines and even online placements offers your target audience invaluable information and you the credibility (trusted consultant), for the reasons explained below.

Although most business owners think of public relations as only being something that larger businesses need to worry about, PR can actually catapult profit margins for a small to medium-sized businesses beyond expectations. For example: producing even a simple press release based on your business can potentially increase Internet rankings, local credibility and lead to an increase in short term sales. PR can be very simple, and with the right guidance can bring about a lot of new interest in your products or services.

The first thing to note about PR and the most common misconception is that businesses thinking about PR need a qualified professional to manage articles and distribution. In reality this is not the case. Yes, it is the better option as these professionals tend to have a contact list of key media types. However, if you become organized by creating a specific action plan of what you want to achieve, then you can actually manage your business PR campaign yourself.

As mentioned before, networking groups are ideal places to meet a variety of different people from various industries. You will however often find attendees involved or have access to journalists, editors or publishers. Remember it is better to be recommended to a fellow business, than to go in blind. If you can, ask your contact to introduce you.

Before approaching these professionals or asking for leads/introductions it is important to plan what objectives you wish to deliver and ensure that your business would benefit from an article. Make sure you plan well, as poorly written articles or spur of the moment requests will often be discarded immediately.

TOP TIP

Do not give people what they want, but instead give them something better.

When creating your "pitch", remember that journalists receive many requests everyday, so there needs to be something within your article that is going persuade the journalist to pick your article in particular to feature. This is why I prefer to call this a pitch because you are effectively "pitch" to the journalist why your article should be chosen above the rest.

Here are a few ideas to consider when looking to utilize PR:

- ✓ Be the first, the newest, the oldest, the biggest, and the smallest: being different is great and the media love it.

- ✓ Introduce something new or improved: Make it clear what's better and why, and what problem it solves over what the rest of the market are offering.

- ✓ Mark the passage of time: Has it been a year, 5 years, or 10 years since something significant happened? Is it your business birthday? Or a certain product's birthday?

- ✓ Announce a new member of your team: Doesn't have to be anyone senior, even junior staff can sometimes make the business pages. Pinpoint the thing that made them the right person for the job and publicize how well they have done. Even better, get them to return to their old local school and tell the senior pupils of their journey.

- ✓ Win an award: Don't just rely on publicity sent by the award organizers, send out your own and add in testimonials.

- ✓ Win a big contract: Don't be afraid to boast – big contracts attract other big contracts. Big businesses are more likely to deal with someone who they believe can deal with similar types of business.

- ✓ Re-launch your website: Tell journalists what's good about your new site and what added functions it has.

- ✓ Offer free information: Free reports like this one are quick and easy to write, and can be incredibly valuable to readers. The years of experience you have in your industry makes you an expert. Journalists and readers appreciate an expert's opinion and may use you for any future articles that require a "trusted consultant" in the future.

✓ Give something free to readers: If you have an actual product, give that away. You can use it to drive traffic from the newspaper to your website. Consider an exclusive deal with one newspaper to get more coverage. Free audio downloads work well or podcasts.

✓ Offer a series of articles: Share your expertise and help a newspaper fill column inches with interesting new content. Don't worry too much about your writing skills, newspapers employ sub-editors to proof any articles that are submitted.

✓ Get involved with a charity: Don't just give cash, that's dull! Instead give your time, product, or better still use your staff and resources to do something exciting and different that will also raise cash for an exciting charity. Painting local hostels at Christmas and supporting local children's charities is a fantastic way to win the hearts and minds of the public. You will find that the local press are keen to support locally based business owners who have the desire to give something back to the local community, especially when it's positive.

> **FACT**
>
> David McConnell named his company Avon after the birthplace of William Shakespeare, Stratford-on-Avon.

If you are fortunate to receive some PR, then ask for an e-copy or pdf download of the article and use it on your website. Editorial coverage gives you credibility especially if written by a publication. It's an independent trusted person giving their opinion about your business that can work as a powerful testimonial, especially those written by governing bodies or trusted organizations such as industry newspapers. It is important to note that some publishers restrict the republication of their material, so it is recommended to ask before assuming you can use their material with your own marketing.

I have talked about the benefits of PR, but it is also very important to know that there can actually be good and bad PR. Bad PR every year affects the success of many small businesses, especially if they're situated in a small-localized area. Because of this, it is imperative that you know how to deal with any negative press and so also possess the vital skill of spinning the negative press into positive.

> "What an immense power over life is the power of possessing distinct aims."
>
> - Elizabeth Stuart Phelps

PR should be thought of as a cost effective way of communicating and advertising to your target market. But again as I keep stressing, it is crucial that you define and pinpoint who your target market is before looking for ways to communicate with them.

Face To A Name – Name To A Face

There is nothing like doing business with someone that you feel you know. This is why many successful entrepreneurs use their own face as a way of branding themselves.

Your clients, like you when you are looking to purchase a product/service, want to know that they are doing business with someone who actually exists and are not just cannon fodder. By using your own face as a marketing piece for your business, you will find that you not only attract more loyal clients, but you also have a better chance of people recognizing you in public. Giving you more opportunities to talk about your business.

"Remember that a person's name is the sweetest and most important sound in any language." This quote comes from Dale Carnegie's book *How To Win Friends And Influence People* which in my opinion was written fifty years ahead of its time. Previously achieving business success was only possible

by adopting a bestselling product or competitive price strategy. However currently, where products can be developed quickly and manufacturing costs can be brought lower thus bringing the overall recommended retail price lower; the key to a successful business is increasingly reliant on brand image and the relationship a business has with its clients. Clients prefer to buy from people, and this never should be forgotten.

> "It's not what you are that holds you back, it's what you think you are not."

— Denis Waitley

Real estate agents are great example of using a face to brand a business, because they work with the public one-on-one and need to be recognized when they're out in public. Many real estate agents will use their face on their business cards, signs and billboards. Although some would call this vain, this is a fundamental part of personal recognition and business success.

Remember, building a business is all about building your reputation and trustworthiness. Even if you don't think you are the most handsome or beautiful person in the World, consider using your face to brand your business. It puts a real person behind a big company name and makes potential clients feel more at ease about doing business with you. My tips to creating the ideal personable image are:

Compose yourself:

It is important to look relaxed and happy in your photo, as this will make sure that you look more human and friendly. Avoid joke pictures, don't pull a face or dress up too much. Just wear what you would normally wear if you wanted to make a good impression.

Get a mix of shots:

Sometimes you can take 100's of photos and only 5 of them are suitable to represent your business. So mix it up, smile, be a little more serious, stand or sit. Some poses will work and some won't; but you won't know until you take the photos and compare them later.

Crop out the boring parts:

You don't want your clients to see that you got the desk you are sitting at from IKEA or that the flowers to the your left are roses! All the focus should be on you. Cut out the bits that could potentially distract your client's attention from yourself. You want your clients to remember your face and not what is behind you!

Hire a photographer:

Always hire a professional that knows how to do the job right. Sometimes it is worth spending the money to ensure you get the best possible picture as just like a logo; these images are likely to be around for a long periods of time. More importantly they are representing your business.

Get feedback:

Show your best shots to some of your clients and get their opinion. Ask them to describe your character just by looking at the photo. It is important to understand that clients will read into an image and take out different opinions. Make sure that these opinions are positive and give the right impression you want to communicate.

Use the same image everywhere:

Once you have decided on the most suitable shot and you have ensured that particular one received the best reviews from your clients; then utilize this picture everywhere. Again just like a logo. Every time a client views that image then the more your brand will be reinforced on their memory.

> "You must begin to think of yourself as becoming the person you want to be."
>
> - David Viscott

From my experience the most effective PR strategies secure a frequent level of media mentions that often only advertising can achieve. By continually monitoring the news cycle and strategically striking while the iron is hot, business can achieve high quality and high quantity media that will help establish and maintain credibility while validating the business's value proposition.

8 - There Is No Such Thing As Luck

8 There Is No Such Thing As Luck

Lucky People Start at 6, Finish at 10

Whenever you hear about someone who is highly successful, it's normally for the wrong reasons. A general word banded around for those who are doing well for themselves is the word "lucky". For me it's the word of doom and one which only "unlucky" people use.

> **" Your attitude, not your aptitude, will determine your altitude. "**
>
> - Zig Ziglar

During a business seminar in 2009, a young man caught my eye through the conference window, he was sitting in a brand new Austin Martin DB9. He could not have been more than 25 years old and was well groomed. I quickly asked the audience to tell me what they saw. After the initial few nervous answers, the delegates started to shout out:

"Must be his dad's car", "He probably won the lottery", "He must be doing something illegal in order to own such a car", "Nice car must have nicked it", "Flash git". Many more slanderous comments continued until one lady said: "He must work harder than us." The room went silent while the remaining delegates processed this information and re-framed their way of thinking. Could it be that this young person actually worked very hard to purchase this car? Could it also be true that he had been "lucky" because of the massive action he had taken within his business to achieve that goal? Although we will never know how he actually came about driving that car; I would prefer to think that his efforts paid off.

In my World, the rule of how lucky you are is simple. Lucky people are those who generally have a better direction about where they are going and will always work (harder) longer hours, hence the title. A great old saying that sums this up in a nutshell is: "The harder I work, the luckier I get." From my experience there is no shortcut to success. Everyone who has become a highly successful entrepreneur has done so by hard work.

ASK YOURSELF

 What do you say to yourself when seeing someone with something you desire? Do you look on and feel a sense of happiness that this must mean that they have achieved, and therefore you must be able to do? Or do you look on with envy?

It's important to note that while working long hours is a must, it doesn't necessarily mean you will be successful. You should only measure your day's work on the amount of "productive work" you have done during this period, not the number of hours that you have been awake. If you spend all of your time surfing the Internet or chatting with friends during long coffee breaks, it's obvious that you are not likely to end up building on your business. Focus in this sense is absolutely vital in achieving your legacy.

TOP TIPS

 Make sure that you appreciate every second you have, because those who have achieved ultimate success know that it arrived because they made every hour and every moment productive.

 Take five minutes out every hour at the same time to break the habit. For example: 10.05 till 10.10, 11.05 till 11.10 and so on.

I cannot emphasise the importance that "lucky" people are merely the ones who make their own luck and therefore achieve success. Luck happens to those who greatly increase the chances of its occurrence. There are very few people in the World that just landed right in the middle of a successful business, especially for not doing very much.

> **"Don't be a spectator, don't let life pass you by."**
>
> - Lou Holtz

Highly successful entrepreneurs are the ones who put the time and forethought into creating a business that will pay them dividends for a lifetime. They don't take shortcuts or try to get out of doing the hard work, they are willing to get in the trenches and do what is required to catapult their business. They spend hours planning processes that will streamline the business in such a way as to create more time for other moneymaking tasks.

Here are several ways in which you can increase your chances of luck:

- ✓ One Goal. It's the most common mistake that business owners make: they try to take on too much, try to accomplish too many tasks at once. It is impossible to maintain energy and focus (the two most important things in accomplishing a goal) if you are trying to do two or more goals at once.

- ✓ Find inspiration. Inspiration can be found in many different ways, but a great place to start to read about those who have already achieved your goals. Use Google or even better use YouTube to see what others have to say.

- ✓ Get excited. This sounds obvious, but most business owners do not think about it: if you want to break out of a negative state, get yourself excited about a goal. This can be done by visualizing and seeing how you will act once you have achieved the task. Start with the end in mind.

- ✓ Build anticipation. This will sound hard, and many business owners will skip this. Start by marking your goal on the calendar. Get excited about that date and decide what you are going to do to celebrate the achievement.

✓ Post your goal. You want to have big reminders about your goal, to keep your focus and keep your excitement going. A picture of your goal helps with this. There are some fantastic tools available on the market including fridge magnets and vision boards; however a cork board will do.

✓ Think about it daily. If you think about achieving your goal every day, it is much more likely to become true. Send yourself daily reminders and commit to doing one small thing daily each day towards your goal.

✓ Build on small successes. Break any big tasks down into smaller steps and complete at least one of these every single day. It may take months or even years to achieve certain tasks, but at least it's a step in the right direction.

✓ Squash negative thoughts; replace them with positive ones. Start monitoring your thoughts and recognize negative self-talk. Change your language patterns from negative to a positive. "I can't do this it's to hard!" and replace it with: "How can I do this and really enjoy the process?"

When you are starting your own business, it's important that you are realistic in the amount of time that you're going to have to work each day to make the business profitable. Most businesses are not an overnight success. It will take a lot of planning as well as trial and error to get a business running. Persistence within business is essential and without it you'll be unable to face challenges. In summary: Lucky people make a point of going out frequently and meeting new people, which increases their chances of having positive encounters. Each one could be life-changing or simply provide good work leads. If you classify yourself as a lucky person, you are much more likely to start conversations with people while standing in a queue. Because you know, whether consciously or not, that the greater the number of contacts you have with others; the more likely it is that one of them will lead to something good.

> TOP TIP

 Think about something that you love doing and the reasons why. Work out a strategy how you can to apply the same level of enthusiasm to your work.

The Support - Getting Someone Better To Do It

One of the biggest mistakes that new business owners make is trying to do everything for themselves as discussed in earlier chapters, it is important to get the best team behind you. We are not all experts at everything we do. As an entrepreneur, it's going to be up to you to figure out where you are the most valuable within your own business, and motivate those within your team to achieve the results that complement your business.

> **ASK YOURSELF**
>
> → What are you really good at within your business?
>
> → Why do people like you?
>
> → What should you not attempt to do?
>
> → How is your time best spent within your business?
>
> → How can you keep in contact on a by-weekly basis with your trusted professionals?

However, empowering others does not just mean employing tactics that persuade other people to your own opinion or goals. It means demonstrating leadership qualities that inspire others to act at their very best, no matter what is asked of them. Such leadership qualities are most in evidence within the armed forces. Soldiers are empowered to greatness by the examples set by their leaders. Sometimes, this can be done by being an admirable and inspirational human being. Of course, some are born with more of these qualities than others, but we can all strive to lead by example, so that others will feel empowered to make great things happen.

Here are some of my recommended tips to get the most from your team. This is by no means a definitive list but key areas that all effective entrepreneurs should hone and develop their skills:

Start as you mean to go on:

When anyone joins your team, you will need to give them time to become fully accustomed to your business. The sooner they settle in, the sooner you can start to reap rewards of their contribution. It will help if you complete an induction and a detailed brief of what you hope to achieve and how they can help. It should outline what you expect from them and within what time scales.

Create realistic expectations:

Strange as it may sound, some professionals do not have a clear sense of their role or what standards they should work to. This is clearly bad for productivity. Your team of trusted professionals need to know their role within your business development and responsibilities.

Review but respect:

Part of motivating your team to work in your best interest is by simply trusting them. Although difficult to do, your team must feel that they can get on with the job. Of course you need to review their work, but there is a happy medium where they know you trust them. Your team is more likely to over-perform if they feel good about what they are doing. Motivated professionals work harder. Trust your gut feeling about your team as it is far easier if the right people are employed in the first place.

Connection and communication:

Effective human connection and communication is the lifeblood of any business, regardless of its size. That means that how you "get on" with your team is essential. This can be done by providing your team with information about what's going on. Occasional e-mails or newsletters to all of those involved within your business (business account managers, accountants, designers, insurance brokers and so on) assist with this; and helps to give them the opportunity to provide you with the most up-to-date industry knowledge.

> "I've got a theory that if you give 100% all of the time, somehow things will work out in the end."
>
> - Larry Bird

Be honest and build trust:

Running a business effectively is not much use if your team of professionals are not getting the whole picture. Bad news is still news, and you must trust that your people are mature enough to give you the best advice no matter what is happening within your business. This does not mean shouting every piece of office gossip from the rooftop, but it does mean keeping your team abreast of all that is relevant to them.

Consultation:

Effective consultation is a vital tool to improving performance. Your team members have specific roles. Your collective overview may be more knowledgeable, but there may be team members whose specific knowledge is greater than yours.

In summary; asking for help within business is not a sign of weakness but a sign of strength. It is sensible to do so and it serves to empower your business. The more facts you have the easier and more effective your business decision will be. In my World, business owners who fail to ask for help are only failing themselves.

Spend Less, Sell More - Bigger Margins, Bigger Balance

Many new business owners in my World, are neglecting to identify areas that potentially can cause their business upset. The primary reason that most small businesses fail within the first six months is due to bad cash management. Too many business owners neglect their cash flow or even identify it until it is too late to recover, and unfortunately are forced to close unnecessarily.

As an entrepreneur it is essential that you learn how to manage your cash flow effectively and establish systems that are easy to manage. In my world, there are several areas that can assist in the successful management of cash flow.

> ### ASK YOURSELF
>
> How will you know that you are managing your cash flow effectively?
>
> How do you know that this is the best way for your business?
>
> Who could you contact for advice?

These areas can massively change the dynamics of your business and the effectiveness of cash flow management. These include: getting the money from clients sooner, paying bills at the last possible moment, concentrating money to a single bank account, managing accounts payable, accounts receivable and inventory more effectively.

Ask for your money/payment:

In your business, you should collect money as fast as you can, other business owners will also be trying to delay payment until it is completely necessary, so just be aware. There are several systems that you can implement to speed up the payments into your account.

- ✓ Speed up online ordering, where clients can order their product anytime anywhere. However when doing so ask them to pay instantly online for the privilege. If they need the product/service fast, then they won't mind paying for it.

- ✓ Send out your invoices the same day goods are shipped or at least once a week. Avoid making accounting a once a month exercise.

- ✓ Indicate on your invoice in BIG LETTERS when payment is due, and specify the penalty interest for late payment.

✓ Ask for credit card details and notify them that the payments will automatically be taken out of their account with any future orders within 7 days.

Don't be fooled that clients or other businesses will not do business with you in the future for chasing payment. From experience those who you want to keep will respect your business efficiency.

Deposit payments immediately:

This seems only obvious, but it's extremely important. Too many business owners sit on payments until they are conveniently going to the bank. If you can, always deposit checks or process payments the same day they are received. Get someone else to do it if you are too busy. Don't hold checks until the next day or the following week, because you lose out on reducing your interest charged if you're in your overdraft.

Ask for immediate availability from the bank:

Each bank has its own availability schedule. Availability is the number of days until you can use the money deposited by cheque as cash. For example, a £1,000 cheque deposited today and assigned one-day availability can be withdrawn as cash tomorrow. Banks availability time varies so make sure you ask when discussing this with your business banking manager.

Incentivise clients who pay early and charge those who don't:

Many people think it is no big deal to neglect accounts receivable until bills are collectible. This is a bad cash flow policy. Motivate clients to pay early by offering them a discount for payments made before the due date. Small discounts such as 5% can cost you less in the long term. Charge a late fee of 3% per month to clients who pay late. If you are unfortunate to get late payers, then make sure you have an automatic system in place, including initial phone calls and then legal letters. These may seem a bit extreme, but the first letter should go out the very day the amount is one day late! After 5 days late, pass over the details to your legal professional to pursue.

Be vigilant and try to get at least periodic payments from slow payers:

Instruct your bank to automatically deposit "returned cheques". Charge back the bank return item fee to your client. Avoid being "too nice" with late payers as once they have found your business boundaries they will use them on all occasions. Be ruthless with your outstanding money.

> **TOP TIPS**
>
> → Do not send out any material if bills remain unpaid.
>
> → Remember that bad debts hurt your bottom line!
>
> → Be aware of large companies that call you out of the blue asking for credit lines or large orders.

In summary, when owed money you must be tough and unrelenting. Adopting this attitude within your business ventures may make the difference between a positive cash flow month and a sluggish month for your business.

Pay your bills at the last minute:

It may seem a bit hypocritical to demand swift payment, and then pay late. But you should never pay a day sooner than you have to, unless you get a discount for doing so. A lot of business owners believe in staying ahead of bills and paying them as early as possible, but that's just poor cash management. You want to keep your money in your hands as long as you can.

You can do this by paying your invoices on the last day they're due, not before. When making your payments always send them on the last day of the month and always on a Friday,. By doing this you allow for delays over the weekend which provides you with that little extra interest.

Have a nil balance if you owe money:

Many businesses make the mistake of keeping too much money in their bank accounts to pay for bank services. This money could be used more effectively elsewhere such as to pay off a loan or to invest at a more competitive rate. Many businesses have no idea how much money to leave in the bank or what alternatives they have to compensate the bank. Take some time to find out what your minimum balance needs to be; and if you need to arrange an overdraft to cater for any immediate payments.

> **TOP TIP**
>
> Use business credit cards for travel, lodging, meals, and small expenses for yourself and your employees. With credit cards you typically don't have to make payment until 25 days after receiving the statement.

In a nutshell, the key to managing a good cash flow is to get your money on time and pay on time. Spend a few moments every month to review your monthly bank statements, (never assume that your bank doesn't make a mistakes), and gauge what steps you can do to run accounting more efficiently.

The Inevitable Feeling Of Being Alone – Home Life

If there is one universal truth that many entrepreneurs live, it is the feeling of being alone. Creative people often work alone in the very beginning as they are building their business from the deep recesses of their own mind.

While there is always stress involved in any job, being an entrepreneur and owner of a business is a highly stressful situation for many people. All of the success or failure of the business rests on your shoulders. That can produce a feeling of loneliness because there really is no one else around you who totally understands what you are going through at any given time.

Fortunately, although it may seem like it, you're not alone. There are plenty of ways to improve your feeling of camaraderie without giving up your hard-won freedom:

Attend business lunches weekly:

A working lunch is a great way to get out of the house to share ideas with friends and fellow business owners. Sure, it's going to take time out of your schedule and will add extra expenses, but the relationships you'll build are worth it.

> " The strongest oak of the forest is not the one that is protected from the storm and hidden from the sun. It's the one that stands in the open where it is compelled to struggle for its existence against the winds and rains and the scorching sun. "

- Napoleon Hill

Get involved with Professional Organizations:

Professional Organizations are full of contacts that have similar interests. Sometimes they offer access to specialized subgroups for colleagues with similar backgrounds. Check out a few meetings as a guest before deciding whether you want to join. If you do, attend all monthly meetings and serve on at least one committee. The more involved you are, the more you'll get back. If you are unsure where to find these groups make a few calls to your trusted consultants and ask them if they can recommend any.

Conventions:

Along with one-day seminars and continuing education courses, conventions provide opportunities to meet other business owners and discuss common problems and strategies. People who attend them usually are interested in exchanging ideas and information, making these events great for building lasting relationships. Scour the local papers and trade magazines; remember to prepare yourself fully before attending.

Rent a desk:

Consider renting a desk space within an existing business. Many small businesses choose to rent space where they can have a small office plus access to a conference room, typing and phone answering service. This can assist with the feeling of not being alone.

"Success" Groups:

As you get to know other entrepreneurs, you can form a weekly or monthly "success" group where you get together and discuss business strategies, problems, sources of new clients, goals or any other issues that you face. Over the years, the members will become trusted confidants who will refer business to each other, brainstorm ideas or provide consolation.

> **More than anything else, I believe it's our decisions, not the conditions of our lives, that determine our destiny.**
>
> - Anthony Robbins

Using these channels, you should be able to recapture that feeling of camaraderie that's been missing, while still maintaining your newfound independence. And besides being a cure for loneliness, they can be great for attracting new business and expanding your network of contacts.

Entrepreneurs typically work very long hours when they are trying to start and run a business They can sacrifice a lot of important family time that they can never get back. This is why it's so important for people to have some kind of balance when it comes to their home life.

Seven common obstacles that entrepreneurs face in living their ideological lives:

1. They generally have difficulty putting themselves first.

2. Their schedule does not reflect their priorities.

3. They feel drained by certain people or things.

4. They feel trapped for monetary reasons.

5. They are living on adrenalin.

6. They don't have a supportive community in their life.

7. Their spiritual well-being comes last.

You may feel that to get ahead or simply maintain your current success you have to work very long hours, sacrificing everything. This is certainly not the case, simply working harder while at work can make a big difference.

TOP TIP

 Avoid getting into the mind-set of believing that if you leave early that your business will fall apart. Delegate well and trust your colleagues.

Entrepreneurs have to learn how to delegate those tasks that can be done by someone else to free themselves up, not only for more time in the business but also for more personal time. It is very easy to burn out as an entrepreneur.

This is because most business owners feel like they have to do everything themselves and be involved in every part of the business. While this may be partially true, it's also important that the business owner takes time out to get a clear head and relax from time to time.

There's an old saying that says: "If an airplane is going down, you must first put the oxygen mask on yourself before you can help someone else." This is exactly the case when it comes to an entrepreneur. If you don't take care of yourself and your own needs, then you will likely lose out on a lot of other parts of your life.

While money and success are very important to many people, it is much more important to maintain a good family life as well. Even if you have all of the success in the World and lose your family life in the process, was it really a success after all? You may still recall the childhood instruction to "be content with what you've got". But consider that every great thing begins as discontent, with a desire for something different.

ASK YOURSELF

 What can you do to identify the "needs" of loved ones?

 How can you implement this within your business planning?

 How can they help to establish this?

There are a few things that entrepreneurs can do in order to help stave off the loveliness that can be felt. For one thing, there must be a specific line of separation between your business and personal life. For instance, turn off your cell phone and computer at a particular time each night no matter what.

If you have children, make a concerted effort to spend more time with them talking or playing. Remember why you're doing what you're doing. If your business is there in order to create more income so that you can enjoy your life and family more, remember those priorities and don't let anything else interfere with it.

In final note your success should not be "at all costs," meaning that you don't want to achieve something if it leaves behind a trail of poor health, ignored spouses and children.

Manage Your Mind, Manage Your Business

Successful entrepreneurs have undoubtable confidence and a strong belief to achieve. Although a misconception, there is nothing mystical about the power of belief. However it is the clear distinction between merely wishing and actually believing which counts. Doubt attracts "reasons" for not succeeding, whereas belief finds the means to achieve.

One of the key tips to avoiding burnout is being able to manage your own mind. Entrepreneurs are very creative people, but they also tend to be very hard on themselves because of their personalities. They can be overly critical and perfectionists.

While these traits are wonderful in certain aspects of business, they can spell disaster for a business owner who doesn't keep a balanced lifestyle. Keeping your mental state balanced each day is very important when it comes to running a business. You cannot get bogged down in petty issues or minute concerns related to the business.

Every great thing starts with a thought and is powered into realization by the belief you have in yourself. Manage your mind well and you shall achieve what you desire sooner than you think. You have to shut your mind down at certain points in order to allow it to rest and relax. This is why the idea of turning off your cell phone and computer at a particular time each night is very important.

Taking some time out to just not think at all is important for all business owners and people in general. Some people do this by meditation, yoga or exercise. Others like to take time out to read a book or take a long walk by the ocean.

TOP TIPS

 Forgive yourself for mistakes as these are undoubtedly going to happen.

 Exercise as often as you can.

 Set a day each month to reward yourself for working hard, and don't miss it no matter what comes up.

Clarity about goals saves a huge amount of energy that can be deployed productively in other areas. No matter what it is that relaxes you, you need to set specific business hours that will be dedicated for work time. Because entrepreneurs love what they do, they assume that there is no need for downtime. They think that they can just keep going and going like the Energizer Bunny without ever taking a break. However, at some point the break will take you. What this means is that your body and mind will require downtime at some point and if you aren't ready for it, it can take you down with it.

> **"Everything you see happening is the consequence of that which you are."**
>
> - David R. Hawkins

Some people end up having anxiety and panic attacks while others start having high blood pressure problems. Not taking time for rest and rejuvenation can have serious physical consequences. It even helps to get out your calendar at the beginning of the month and set aside a few days that will be personal days. You can vow that you will not be accessible by phone, e-mail or any other way on those days. Have people in place that can support you by taking care of business while you take time to rejuvenate.

Wealth Is Good, So Enjoy It – Make Happiness A Present

The Chinese character for wealth is composed of two symbols: a seashell, an ancient symbol of trade. As well as a symbol that literally translated means "brilliance," but implies the uniqueness that each of us has in terms of a talent or ability. Wealth therefore comes from selling what is unique about you (in terms of a product or just you as a person).

Although money itself is a mystery, whatever best expresses your brilliance will inevitably lead you to wealth. It will free you from poverty and give you a mindset that attracts abundance. Being rich means nothing if you never get to enjoy it. How many people do we all know who seem to work all the time, burning the candle at both ends, and never have time to enjoy it? You will often hear people say that at the end of their life, they don't believe that they will think they wish they had more time for work.

While work is important and a necessity for most people, it is not LIFE. You must make an effort to enjoy the fruits of your labour. If you work and work, the money is not what will make you happy. The enjoyment of the money is the key to happiness.

> **ASK YOURSELF**
>
> → How can you enjoy the newly found wealth and abundance?
>
> → When will you know that you have achieved it?
>
> → How can you ensure that this is going to happen within the time scale?
>
> → What massive action are you taking today to work towards it?

Use your newfound wealth as a way to enjoy your life more. For some people, this means taking time to travel to new places. For other people, this means participating more in a favourite hobby such as playing golf. By living with more vitality and happiness, you will also help to keep your mind balanced.

It all works in a circle. The more you work, the wealthier you become. The wealthier you become, the more you can pursue happiness. The more you pursue happiness, the better you are able to work. Decide what truly will make you happy, aside from just money. Money, in and of itself, will not make you happy. Using the money in a specific way is what will make you happy. Perhaps you want to give more to charity or start your own foundation. Maybe you want to fund mission trips or support children in underprivileged nations. These are all ways to create more happiness in your life by giving to others.

> **" You can kill a man but you can't kill an idea. "**
>
> - Medgar Evers

While money cannot buy happiness, it can buy other things which lead to happiness. It can buy more time, for instance. More time allows you to have more fun with family and friends. Money also buys freedom. It allows you to free yourself from the shackles of a 9 to 5 job or a terrible employer. However, if an entrepreneur is not careful, he or she can become shackled just as easily to their own business.

TOP TIP

 Put aside at least 10 percent of your earnings and mark that off as "not for expenditure." Over time this amount builds and starts earning money for you, without you having to do any work. It matters little how much you start with, as long as you observe the rule to pay yourself first out of whatever you earn. You will soon not even notice the absence of this small amount.

Money buys things that can add happiness to your life such as a nicer car, bigger home or that cool motorcycle you had been eyeing since your were 16 years old. These things can bring joy and happiness. Money allows you to have more experiences like seeing the great pyramids in Egypt or taking a cruise around the world. Perhaps you get to eat at the finest dining establishments in your area or see your favourite local sporting events. These experiences also allow you to connect with others and rejuvenate yourself.

> **Conflict cannot survive without your participation.**
>
> - Wayne Dyer

In summary, money can relieve some stress. It can keep your bills paid and cover your basic living expenses. It can pay off debt and free the stress from your mind associated with it. Even though money can do all of these things, true long-lasting happiness comes from loving what you do and using your wealth in a responsible way.

Rewarding Yourself For Doing Good- Smile

It is so important that you not take yourself or your business so seriously that you cannot reward yourself for a job well done. Take time to stop and appreciate where you came from and how far you have gotten since you started. Learn to smile and be grateful for what you have achieved.

When you set goals in your business, make sure that you reward yourself when you accomplish one of your goals. Treat yourself to something that you would enjoy. It doesn't have to cost a lot of money and can actually be something quite creative. It might just be a day off, a bubble bath or a big bowl of ice cream. No matter what, it's important to acknowledge for yourself that you did something good.

It might be helpful to create a list of rewards at the very beginning of your goal setting process. That way, you can pick from the list of rewards when you have achieved something.

Remember that rewards should be something to nourish your body and soul and sustain you through those periods where you feel like you aren't making any progress. You may want to create a set of immediate rewards, medium-term and long-term ones.

TOP TIPS

 Once you have achieved, you are more likely to achieve again because you now have it in you to succeed.

 When taking time out, turn off all communication and let your clients know that this will be a standard procedure during these times.

The most effective reward that I have used in the past is to reward yourself with time. Time away without any interruptions, mobile phones, Internet connections or e-mail access. Although this takes some discipline and will likely be hard for the first few days, it can radically change the values you have towards your business.

This time away should be considered as a break from "thought". These "thought" holidays are ways of rewarding yourself for the hard work. Many top entrepreneurs abide by the saying, "Work hard, play harder." It's a chance for them to feel the rewards of their hard work. Sure, lavish trips and spending may not be your way of playing hard. Make sure to reward yourself with something that you can truly appreciate, such as time, and this makes perfect sense. Within your business it's likely that you do not have enough time to complete all of the things that you want to. Time therefore is always something that is of ultimate value.

In summary, taking a break from work also puts everything into perspective. It gives you time to reflect and learn from the process: your right decisions, some wrong ones, and mistakes that you should swear to avoid making in the future.

Put Something Back - Share Your Knowledge With Others

Many people believe in the idea of karma which basically means that what goes around comes around. In other words, what you give out is what you get back eventually. This is also true when it comes to the business world.

Those entrepreneurs who give back to their community and to those around them typically get that back one hundred fold. But it's not just about giving back to the community as much as it is about giving back to the generations that are coming next. It's important to put something back by sharing your knowledge with other people. This might be done through a networking group or by simply allowing college students to intern at your business.

> ### TOP TIP
> Set some personal goals about giving back or sharing knowledge with others.

You might decide to speak at a local school or club to share your knowledge about business and entrepreneurialism. There are many different ways that you can give back to future generations who want to be business owners just like you did. It is critical that you never forget your own roots and where you came from before you were a success.

Whenever you hear of someone who's been very successful in business, inevitably there was someone at the beginning of that chain reaction who helped that person believe in themselves. You can do that too, and in fact you should do that. Giving back is one of the most important factors in the overall success of the business person.

Never hold on to all of the knowledge that you have without sharing it with others. Be willing to be open and honest to help other people gain a level of success as you have. By sharing your own knowledge, you will lay the foundation for future generations of quality business people and leave a legacy that can never be erased.

Work for your own success, but ensure that your achievements lift up the wider community. In other words, recognize and use your background in the service of attaining your goals, and remember to give something back.

"Everyone needs to be valued. Everyone has the potential to give something back."

- Princess Diana

Not The End
But
The Beginning

Benjamin's Top Tips To Being An Effective Entrepreneur

✓ Dedicate your life to continuous learning and never-dying curiosity of betterment.

✓ A compelling vision: Entrepreneurs define their reality (what they believe is possible), then set about "managing their dream" by taking massive action.

✓ Share development with others and communicate that vision, in doing so others follow it.

✓ Tolerating uncertainty and taking on risk, understand that the only risk is not taking it.

✓ Entrepreneurs must have outstanding personal integrity, self-knowledge and maturity.

✓ Invest in increasing in knowledge of life. You can't afford not to.

✓ Entrepreneurs learn from others, but are not made by others.

✓ Reinvention: to create new things sometimes involves recreating yourself. You may be influenced by your genes and environment, but leaders take all their influences and create something unique.

✓ Taking time off to think and reflect, which brings answers and produces resolutions.

✓ Passion for the promises of life: a belief in the best, for yourself and others.

✓ Seeing success in small, everyday increments and joys, not waiting years for the Big Success to arrive.

✓ Service is the key to success. Don't just sell things; find out what people really want. This requires greater than normal thought and observation.

ENTREPRENEURS ALWAYS DRIVE ON EMPTY

The *Ultimate* Business Bible

Over the last 10 years Benjamin Bonetti, serial entrepreneur and successful Business Coach, has assisted and guided *thousands* of entrepreneurs and business owners through their journey for success.

His advice is *highly respected* within the business community with regular appearances on T.V. and Radio as a Celebrity Life Coach, Motivational Expert and Business Guru. Bonetti's internationally acclaimed *sell out* seminars are regularly attended by savvy entrepreneurs; many of which owe Bonetti's inspiration to their own massive success.

Within this book Bonetti has included his "never heard before" secrets, theories and psychological techniques that have massively changed the dynamics of thousands of business ventures, from small businesses to major corporations.

If you think it's *your* time to massively improve the quality of your personal and professional life and attract money, fulfilment and recognition; then this book can truly show you how!

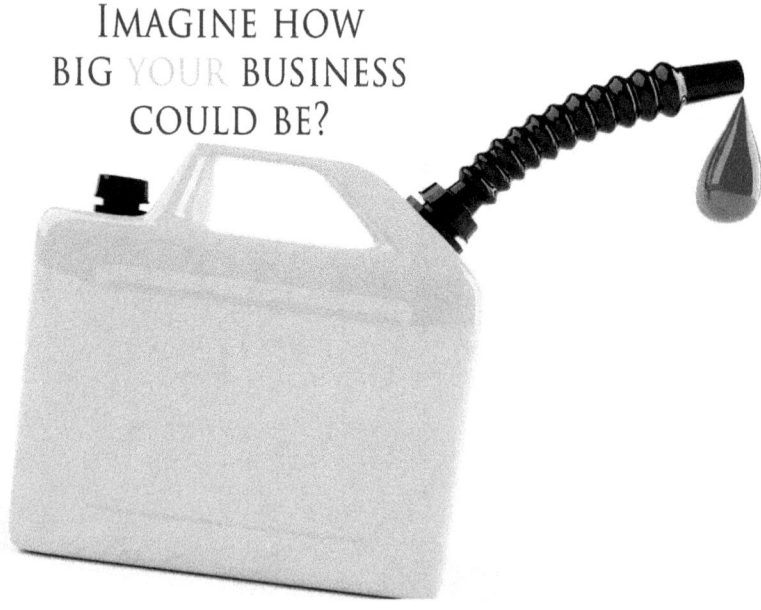

IMAGINE HOW BIG YOUR BUSINESS COULD BE?

www.ingramcontent.com/pod-product-compliance
Lightning Source LLC
Chambersburg PA
CBHW051641170526
45167CB00001B/280